ROSE HILL

MVFOL

ROSE HILL

An Intermarriage before Its Time

Carlos E. Cortés

Heyday, Berkeley, California
Inlandia Institute, Riverside, California

The publisher would like to thank the James Irvine Foundation for their support of Inland Empire literature.

This Inlandia book was published by Heyday and Inlandia Institute.

Library of Congress Cataloging-in-Publication Data
Cortés, Carlos E.
 Rose Hill : an intermarriage before its time / Carlos E. Cortés.
  p. cm.
 ISBN 978-1-59714-188-8 (pbk. : alk. paper) -- ISBN 978-1-59714-190-1 (ebook)
 1. Cortés, Carlos E. 2. Kansas City (Mo.)—Ethnic relations. 3. Mexican Americans—Missouri—Kansas City—Biography. 4. Jews—Missouri—Kansas City—Biography. 5. Interethnic marriage—Missouri—Kansas City. 6. Interfaith marriage—Missouri—Kansas City. 7. Kansas City (Mo.)—Biography. I. Title.
 F474.K29A24 2012
 305.8009778'411--dc23
                        2011038936

Chapter 10 contains a quote from a United States Air Force fact sheet, from the Office of Public Affairs, 509th Bomber Wing, Whiteman AFB, Missouri.

Cover Art: Background photo, "In the Garden of Dead: Two of a Kind" by
  Jadwiga Nycz, 2009, www.flickr.com/photos/violen.
Cover Design: Lorraine Rath
Interior Design/Typesetting: Rebecca LeGates
Printed and bound by Worzalla, Stevens Point, Wisconsin

Orders, inquiries, and correspondence should be addressed to:
  Heyday
  P.O. Box 9145, Berkeley, CA 94709
  (510) 549-3564, Fax (510) 549-1889
  www.heydaybooks.com

10 9 8 7 6 5 4 3 2 1

For Mom and Dad.

Contents

PROLOGUE

1

A Couple before Their Time

Dad was a Mexican Catholic. Mom was a Kansas City–born Jew with Eastern European immigrant parents. They fell in love in Berkeley, California, and got married in Kansas City, Missouri.

That alone would not have been a big deal. But it happened in 1933, when such marriages were rare. And my parents spent most of their lives in Kansas City, a place both racially segregated and religiously divided.

Mom and Dad chose to be way ahead of their time; I didn't. But because of them, I had to be. My mixed background meant that, however unwillingly, I had to learn to live as an outsider.

2

Rose Hill

Today they all lie quietly in Kansas City's Rose Hill Cemetery—
Mom, Dad, Grandma, Granddad. Maybe I shouldn't say quietly.
If the dead can bicker, they're probably still at it.

Someday I'll join them at Rose Hill, but I probably won't die
in Kansas City, as they did. When I left home in 1952, it was for
good. More precisely, it was for life, since I, too, have a Rose Hill
plot.

I hope they are at peace at Rose Hill, a peace they seldom
found while they were alive. Conflict was the norm in my family.
I lived with it growing up, and even after moving away, I continued to be part of it. I still feel it when I go out to Rose Hill to visit
my family's graves. Conflict is part of my story.

My story of a childhood spent in a constant crossfire—straddling borders, balancing loves and loyalties, and trying to fit into
a world that wasn't quite ready for someone with a Mexican Catholic father and a Jewish American mother. My story of conflicted
choices about my personal survival and happiness, even while
knowing that some of my decisions would bring pain to those
who loved and raised me. And my story of how I finally grew to
develop greater compassion for my family and a better understanding of myself in the more than half century since I left Kansas City.

It hasn't been an easy story to figure out, nor an easy one to tell.
I hope it's all true, Scout's Honor.

FROM DIFFERENT WORLDS

3

Brunhilde and the Oilman

Dad was the first Mexican that Mom had ever met. It happened in 1932 in Berkeley, where she was a senior at the University of California.

Four years earlier, Dad, too, had graduated from Cal (in those days referred to as Cal only, never as UC Berkeley). He had spent his freshman year at the University of Nevada in Reno, where he boxed and played football. Then his father came down with colon cancer, dying in 1928. As the oldest son with five younger siblings, Dad felt special family responsibilities. So he returned to Berkeley, where his family was living, to finish college and start work on an M.A. in history.

Then the Great Depression hit. Historians not being in great demand, Dad took a job in a gas station, and had moved up to assistant manager before he met Mom in the fall of 1932. By January 1933 they had decided to get married.

Mom and Dad made an attractive couple. Only about five foot eight, and shaped more like a stump than a tree, Dad had a hunkish face, twinkling eyes, and charm in abundance when he decided to turn it on. About an inch shorter than Dad, Mom wasn't traditionally pretty, but she was striking, with an effervescence that could both captivate and irritate.

Mom and Dad enjoyed telling stories of their courtship. How Mom literally fell for Dad, tripping on her sorority house stairs and plopping in front of him on their first (blind) date. How Dad had nicknamed her Brunhilde, both because of her love for German opera and because she weighed 180 pounds, nearly as much as he did. How Dad adored her voice and encouraged her to pursue a singing career (at his urging, she tried out for and won a leading role in the annual Cal spring musical).

They also used those brief months of courtship to share their families' pasts, at great length. This meant talking about the differences in their backgrounds and how those differences might affect their lives. But maybe they didn't talk enough. Or maybe no amount of talking could have fully prepared them for the conflicts that their future would bring.

4

Dad's Mexican Family

Even with grime under his fingernails, Dad enchanted Mom with stories about his aristocratic ancestry.

He told her that he was descended from the Hernán Cortés extended family that came to Mexico as conquistadores in the early sixteenth century. That his ancestors included members of many of Mexico's elite families—landowners, politicians, ambassadors, priests, generals. That some family members had fought with fabled Mexican President Benito Juárez in the mid-nineteenth-century War of the Reform, while others fought against him. That some served Mexico's Emperor Maximilian during his short, turbulent reign in the 1860s, while others battled to overthrow him.

Then came the Mexican election of 1910. My grandfather, also Carlos Cortés like both Dad and me, joined the presidential campaign of his personal friend Francisco Madero against longtime strongman President Porfirio Díaz. Because Díaz controlled the electoral machinery, he inevitably won.

His victory triggered the Mexican Revolution, leading to the overthrow of Díaz and the installation of Madero as president. Granddad—a haughty, imposing, barrel-chested landowner with piercing black eyes, ebony hair, and an enormous, upturned handlebar moustache—became Madero's *jefe político* (political boss) of Guadalajara, Mexico's second-largest city.

This was well and good, until General Victoriano Huerta overthrew the revolutionary government and, in 1913, assassinated Madero. When Granddad learned that he, too, was on Huerta's hit list, he and Grandma fled to the United States, settling in Berkeley near her family.

Despite the loss of his possessions, Granddad had something that tens of thousands of other Mexican Revolution refugees lacked—a college education. With an engineering degree from Stanford and fluency in English, he was able to find a good job with Shell Oil.

But there was one final glitch in my family's escape from Mexico. When Granddad and Grandma Cortés fled, they took all of their children with them except Dad. Just six years old, Dad was left in Guadalajara with his father's fiercely religious sister, Anita. For five years, until Dad rejoined his family in California in 1918, Tía Anita immersed him in Catholicism and fostered in him what would become a passionate pride in being Mexican.

I'm not sure why my grandparents left Dad behind; different stories have been passed down through various members of our extended family. That their fake passport and travel documents listed one too few children, so one child had to be left behind. That my granddad wanted Dad to provide companionship for Anita, who remained in Guadalajara. Or that Huerta's hit men were waiting at Dad's school to arrest and execute Granddad when he came to pick little Carlos up, forcing the family to flee immediately without him.

The latter was Dad's version of the story, which he loved to tell because it was so dramatic. But beneath the sense of drama and adventure, there was often a touch of resentment about the family going off without him, as if he believed they could have somehow found a way to take him. And there was a sense that he had lost out on something vitally important, those five crucial formative years with his siblings.

In fleeing to the United States, my family lost just about everything—everything, that is, except memories of being part of the Mexican aristocracy. Those memories nourished Dad, particularly when he later moved to Kansas City and once again became isolated from his family, who ultimately scattered throughout Mexico and California.

Telling me family stories—over and over—helped Dad hang on to his sense of being. But those memories also wrapped him in a time warp. As the years went by, this solitary, dislocated Mexican aristocrat increasingly found himself trapped in the wrong time and place.

5

Dad's Mother

Dad also told Mom about his mother's family. This story was his ace in the hole, helping him overcome Mom's religious reservations about their getting married.

Dad couldn't avoid the fact that he had been raised Catholic by his devoutly religious aunt. But he could—and did—point out that his mother, Reine, was Jewish, the US-born descendant of a nineteenth-century French immigrant, Simon Blum, who became a prosperous San Francisco Bay Area merchant.

When my Grandfather Cortés met Reine Blum, he was a student at Stanford. They married in San Francisco, where Dad was born in 1907 shortly before they returned to Mexico.

I loved Dad's tale of my grandparents' courtship. Carlos and Reine met while serving as volunteers in an emergency tent city following the 1906 San Francisco earthquake. This was one of Dad's favorite stories, and for years I repeated it, sometimes in my classes and public lectures. One day, I bothered to check their wedding date, only to discover that they were married *prior* to the earthquake. I'm glad I didn't learn this until after Dad's death. I wouldn't have wanted to destroy one of those tenuous threads of memory that kept him going.

Although Dad was raised deeply Catholic while he lived with his Guadalajara aunt, Tía Anita, Mom dug her teeth into Reine's Jewish ancestry. According to Jewish law (Halakha), religious identity is passed down to children through their mother. So Mom insisted that Dad had to be Jewish, too, regardless of how he was raised, what he believed, or where he worshiped.

Dad's mother became Mom's weapon when she tried to convince her anguished Jewish immigrant parents that they should accept a Mexican Catholic as their son-in-law. After all, he was *really* Jewish.

Mom's mother, my Grandma Hoffman, later adopted this incantation—"he's really Jewish"—and invoked it during times of heated family conflict. Mom and Grandma repeated it endlessly, as if it could wash away Dad's Catholic lineage and rearing. But I don't think either of them ever actually believed it. And I know damn well Granddad Hoffman didn't, because he often and angrily told me so.

These religious dynamics all became clearer during my high school years, when I began to pry into family secrets and tensions. In bursts of (sometimes drunken) honesty, Mom would spill her true feelings, as well as Grandma Hoffman's. Granddad Hoffman was far too direct and guileless to ever play the "he's really Jewish" game.

But I wonder if Mom would have ever had the courage to try to sell Dad to her folks if Dad's mother had *not* been Jewish.

6

Mom's Folks

Mom didn't have as much to tell Dad about her heritage. She talked about her extended families—the Hoffmans (Granddad) and the Weinsafts (Grandma)—clustered mainly in Kansas City, a prime destination for Jewish immigrants. But she didn't know a great deal about their European backgrounds, except that they came to the United States around the turn of the century. Neither Grandma nor Granddad was willing to share much more.

Aside from being immigrants, Mom's family was everything that Dad's family wasn't. Dad came from an elite background; Mom's heritage was working class. Dad's parents were well educated; Mom's didn't finish elementary school. Dad's folks were well read; Mom's folks seldom read, at least for pleasure. And while Dad reveled in his Mexican heritage, Grandma and Granddad Hoffman essentially buried their European pasts, passing on little of their families' histories. And for good reason.

It wasn't easy being Jewish in nineteenth-century eastern Europe. Anti-Semitism smoldered continuously and erupted periodically in individual incidents and widespread pogroms that decimated Jewish villages and disrupted Jewish lives. This was a world my grandparents had left behind. It was too damn painful for them to talk about.

According to conflicting accounts in family lore, Morris Hoffman (my grandfather) was born in either Belarus or Ukraine, maybe near Kiev, maybe near Odessa. His death certificate merely says "Russia."

Like tens of thousands of other Jews, the Hoffmans fled to the United States. Granddad's parents, along with others of the Hoffman clan, came first. Granddad Hoffman followed, arriving in New York at age sixteen. There he found work in a New York City restaurant, sleeping on the restaurant floor until he could save up enough money to rejoin his parents in Kansas City.

Ada Weinsaft (my grandmother) was born in Vienna. Her family fled Austria so that the Weinsaft boys wouldn't have to serve in the military. They, too, settled in Kansas City, with its growing, close-knit Jewish community.

It was there that the Hoffmans linked up with the Weinsafts— or at least one handsome, broad-shouldered young Hoffman, Morris, met one beautiful, delicate young Weinsaft, Ada. They courted mainly in Yiddish, the common language of Eastern European Jews, and were married while in their teens in a Reform Jewish temple.

With limited means and little education, Grandma and Granddad worked tirelessly to become middle class. First they ran a small grocery store and sold produce together in the Kansas City market. Then Grandma managed apartments and a hotel so Granddad could go to night school. Finally, in 1921, the year after they became naturalized US citizens, Granddad started his own little construction business.

But this effort wasn't just for the two of them. It was also for little Florence, my mother, their only child, born in 1912. (Though she was born Frieda Florence, Mom detested her first name and, displaying the stubbornness that would characterize her life, insisted on being called Florence, later changing her name officially.)

Mom was Grandma and Granddad's hope, their future. They sacrificed so that Mom could have opportunities they never had. Piano and singing lessons, which led her to dream of an operatic career. A first year of college at Ward Belmont, a private women's school in Nashville. Finally, three years at the University of California, Berkeley, before she was to return to Kansas City, presumably to marry her longtime Jewish boyfriend.

So I can hardly imagine the shock and pain Grandma and Granddad Hoffman must have felt when they received Mom's January 1933 letter, midway through her senior year at Berkeley, informing them that she had fallen in love with a Mexican Catholic immigrant named Carlos Cortés, who worked in a service station. But, of course, he was really Jewish.

7

Watchful Eyes

After receiving Mom's letter, Grandma Hoffman took the train out to Berkeley, where she rented an apartment for several months in order to get a close look at this Mexican who had intruded on their lives. At first she tried to talk Mom out of marrying him, but she soon realized that there was no bend in her willful daughter, whose determination often became obstinacy. So Grandma pulled back and tried to establish a relationship with Dad. Grandma always hedged her bets, taking great care to avoid appearing an obstructionist.

Less flexible but more prescient, Granddad, too, had serious reservations about his daughter's marriage. Dad could be disarmingly charming when he wanted to be, which got him to at least first base with Grandma. But from his distant perch in Kansas City, hardened by his fierce Eastern European Jewish sense of distrust born of a painful history, Granddad was immune to those charms.

He dearly loved Mom and feared, quite reasonably, that this unimaginable marriage across religious and ethnic lines would lead to trouble for his little girl. So, after learning from Grandma that Mom was determined to marry this Mexican, Granddad wrote two letters, one to Mom and one to Dad. I have the letter he wrote to Mom:

It is natural that Mother and I want to be very sure that Carlos is the right man, that he is worthy of our daughter whom we love better than our own lives and for whom we have made great personal sacrifices in order to give her opportunities for education and culture, which we were denied in our youth.…After all dear heart you have been carefully reared in our house by a great and wonderful Mother and you are worthy in choosing your own husband and we trust in your judgment and I pray to God that you are making the right step.

At a family dinner some ten years ago, I read the full letter to my daughter, Alana, and her cousins, my brother Gary's three kids, all in their thirties. They laughed and said Granddad was laying a guilt trip on Mom.

This may seem so when viewed through contemporary eyes. But Gary and I didn't laugh. We could feel the anguish of this proud, dignified, unlettered immigrant, who closely guarded his emotions. We could sense his desperation as he struggled to find the right words to express what was in his heart. Granddad's letter combined passion with paternalism, support with possessiveness, disappointment with protectiveness, and love with dread.

I never read his other letter, the one to Dad. My brother, Gary, and his wife, Debby, found it, but it disappeared when their basement flooded. They remember the letter differently; Debby recalls Granddad threatening Dad that he had better take good care of his only daughter, while Gary remembers it as a warning not to marry his daughter.

However it read, Dad knew that he was not warmly embraced. But he may not have realized that he was permanently on probation.

8

A Wedding of Compromises

Shortly after Mom graduated from Cal in May 1933, she and Grandma returned by train to Kansas City. Two months later, Dad took the train to Kansas City for their wedding.

Missouri was not a hospitable place for people of color. It had rigid legal segregation, including an anti-miscegenation law that barred marriages between "white people" and those with "Negro blood." Blacks were segregated in the northeast part of Kansas City, while most Mexicans lived on the Westside near downtown.

But to hell with Kansas City's racial traditions. Mom insisted that she was going to marry her Mexican love, and stubbornly resisted her folks' entreaties to wait longer before getting married.

Dad, too, confronted family opposition. Despite her Jewish heritage—or maybe because of it—Dad's mother mirrored the Hoffmans in her lack of enthusiasm for the marriage. In fact, neither she nor any of Dad's five brothers and sisters attended the wedding.

A major hiccup in the wedding preparations became the choosing of a best man. Dad didn't know anybody in Kansas City, but he did have one midwestern friend, Paul Markham, who lived in Omaha. So Dad invited Paul to be his best man.

Paul also happened to be Gentile. When Dad wrote to Mom about his choice and she relayed it to her folks, Grandma (according to Mom) nearly suffered a nervous breakdown. So Mom asked Dad to disinvite Paul.

Dad agreed, but only if Mom would be willing to back down on one of her suggestions—that they get married on her Daddy's birthday, July 18. This ominous Sophoclean suggestion both irritated Dad and gave him a sense of foreboding. He wasn't about to share his wedding day with "Daddy." And he had a premonition, an all-too-accurate one, that he was embarking on an eternal competition for Mom's love and loyalty.

So both Mom and Dad won...and lost. For best man, Mom recruited one of her uncles. Dad hadn't even met him. And they got married by a rabbi on July 16, not on "Daddy's birthday," as my father derisively referred to the wedding date that never was. With this embattled exchange, my family established a tradition of ethno-religious compromises, often bizarre ones, and launched a half-century clash of cultures.

The wedding also gave Dad the opportunity to initiate what would become a lifetime of guerrilla warfare with the Hoffman-Weinsaft clan. Just before he left for Kansas City, Dad was told he needed glasses, and when he arrived he was wearing them—for the first time in his life. He hadn't bothered to inform Mom.

Dad wore his glasses the entire time he was in Kansas City. Despite Mom's pleading, he refused to take them off, even for the wedding pictures. Then, during their honeymoon, he accidentally broke his glasses. And he didn't replace them. It would be twenty years before he again started wearing glasses.

Mom swore that Dad did all of this on purpose. During her rants, Dad would say nothing, but would merely look at me with a shit-eating grin.

The wedding, however, came off. Grandma informed the *Kansas City Jewish Chronicle* that Dad was an oilman from California. The newspaper misspelled Dad's last name—"Cortez" with a *z*, not the correct "Cortés" with an *s*. It wouldn't be the last time for him, or for me.

THE JOURNEY BEGINS

9

Dreams Deferred

Mom and Dad had lots of dreams. Dad dreamed of getting his own service station. Then, someday, when they could afford it, he would complete his M.A., become a high school history teacher, and write. Mom dreamed of an operatic career. But those dreams would have to wait.

For one of the few times in my life, I showed up early. Just nine months after their wedding, I joined the family prematurely (by ten days) in Oakland, California, on April 6, 1934.

My unplanned arrival didn't help financially. Nor did it help logistically, since Dad's family didn't provide much of a support network. Six months later, Mom and Dad moved to Kansas City so Grandma Hoffman could help take care of little Carlos.

For several years we barely made it. Dad bounced from job to job, trying to bring home enough money for essentials. Sometimes not enough.

Grandma couldn't sit by and watch her only child and grand-child do without. So during the day, while Dad was at work, she would bring over food, clothes, and other necessities, always in small amounts to try to conceal things from Dad. Too smart not to notice, but also too needy to refuse, and too proud to admit it, Dad said nothing. Self-deception became a permanent member of our family.

Once, when I was sick, the doctor refused to see me because we hadn't paid our medical bill. Mom called Dad, who came home, telephoned the doctor, and told him he was bringing me down, threatening to beat the hell out of him if he didn't see me. When they got me there, the doctor had left. Another doctor treated me.

I heard that story many times, always from Mom. I don't know if it's true. But whenever Mom would tell it, Dad would purse his lips, smile sheepishly, and get a mischievous glint in his eyes.

Dad finally got a steady job selling tires for Firestone. And we welcomed a new family member, my little brother Gary, in December 1939.

Then World War II broke out. It would completely change our lives.

10

World War II

December 7, 1941, provided my first vivid memory. We were out in our backyard, with music on the radio, when the program was interrupted by news that Japan had bombed Pearl Harbor. That didn't mean much to a seven-year-old, but Mom's tears did.

She burst into tears again later that week when Dad mentioned, almost offhandedly, that he was joining the navy. Fortunately for us, he got turned down.

A year earlier Dad had fallen off a ladder, badly injuring his leg. When incipient gangrene set in, the doctor recommended amputation. But Dad, a human bulldog, refused to surrender his leg, despite the doctor's warning that the condition might kill him. And it might have eventually, since circulatory problems would plague him for the rest of his life. However, emphysema and Parkinson's got to him first, forty-five years later.

Just in case, Dad insisted on giving confession and taking last rites from a priest. This disconcerted Grandma and Granddad Hoffman, because it suggested that he wasn't really Jewish.

Because the navy didn't want my gimpy father, he was still in Kansas City the next year when the army decided to build the Sedalia Glider Base sixty-five miles southeast of Kansas City, near Knob Noster, Missouri. The base would be used to help train troops for the invasion of Europe. Granddad bid on part of the construction.

It was an enormous gamble. Granddad's tiny construction company could only handle as many small jobs as Granddad, alone, could supervise personally. He had never taken on a project anywhere near this size.

Although there were no other bidders, the government was leery about awarding him the contract. Finally, faced with the reality of supply and demand, the government relented. But Grandma and Granddad had to pledge their home as a guarantee that he would complete the job on time. If he didn't, he would incur huge penalties. At fifty-two, he could have lost everything.

Almost out of desperation, Granddad asked Dad to become his transportation superintendent on the Knob Noster project. This meant Dad would have to give up his Firestone job and put the entire family at risk.

Despite these serious reservations, and impelled by Mom, Dad joined Granddad in the perilous venture, and my family became part of the army of 2,500 workers who helped build the glider base during the summer of 1942. My grandparents rented a house in Warrensburg, a few miles from Knob Noster, so Granddad and Dad could be near the job.

How well I remember the summer of 1942, especially the weather. According to a latter-day air force fact sheet, "During those dry summer months, the dust was so bad that the early employees of the field found it almost impossible to see in front of their cars as they approached the field to go to work." Occasional pounding rains made things worse, periodically turning the construction site into a quagmire.

On weekends Mom would take us over to Warrensburg. Most of the family conversations concerned problems with the job. Then there were those long silences at the dinner table while the weather gods diddled with our family's fate. Even Granddad, generally so confident and stalwart, was muted by the extended periods of challenging weather.

But the gamble paid off. In fact, Granddad and Dad finished the job ahead of schedule. So proud they were. Granddad even received letters commending him for his contributions to the war effort.

And their success also helped them personally. Granddad's business took off and Dad agreed to stay on with the company.

By then we had bought our first home, in the south part of Kansas City. We were slowly moving up, economically. But that decision—that Dad would remain in Granddad's business—also put us on a new family trajectory.

11

The Business

After Knob Noster, Granddad, Dad, and Mom (now the company office manager) immersed themselves in the business; it became the center of our family.

Not that my family was all business. Sometimes it just seemed that way. We had lots of family fun on outings at the amusement park, the zoo, and the municipal ballpark. There were long stays at Grandma and Granddad's summer home at Lake Lotawana, some thirty miles from Kansas City. Things were fine as long as we were on the move or with friends or among extended family. But when just the six of us settled down together, as during our frequent family dinners, the business almost inevitably moved to front and center.

Neither reserved, intellectual Dad nor stolid, formal Granddad were much at casual gab. Grandma and Mom could converse with the best of them, but it was mainly small talk, with Mom doing most of the heavy lifting to keep all of us involved. Except for a few topics, like baseball and classical music, my folks didn't share many interests with my grandparents, and underlying cultural tensions placed some topics, like ethnicity and religion, off-limits.

Moreover, Mom, Dad, and Granddad saw each other nearly every day at work and lunch, so family conversations soon reached their limits. It was only a matter of time until somebody would ask a question about the business—the progress of some job, a bid that had to be submitted, the need to make personnel shifts, or other topics that I found, well, less than fascinating. They may have interpreted my silence as interested listening, since it was generally assumed that I would ultimately join the business. They were wrong, on both counts.

12

Granddad Hoffman

I can't recall ever seeing Granddad really smile. I know he found pleasures in life, like Kansas City Philharmonic concerts, or when Mom sang a long solo in the Temple B'nai Jehudah choir, or when Gary won some athletic award, or when I came home with straight A's, or when elegant Grandma was particularly charming with their Saturday night poker club.

I could tell when Granddad was happy because of an occasional slight upturn at the corner of his mouth, or the rare glint in his eyes behind those steel-rimmed glasses. It's just that this glint seldom migrated to other parts of his face, or softened his guttural voice. And he almost never laughed.

Tension often accompanied Granddad into a room. Others—friends and relatives— found him disconcerting. My niece, Rita, who was seven when he died, recalls him as a "big, scary guy." Only about five foot ten, he loomed much larger, his air of austere mysteriousness heightened by his heavy Slavic accent. Almost nobody—not even business associates—called him by his first name, "Morris." It was always "Mr. Hoffman."

Mom and Dad would tell Gary and me stories about his flashing temper and tyrannical style. Granddad and Dad often fought at the office, or so Dad said, but at family gatherings, one intense Granddad glare could drive Dad into his shell of smoldering silence. Most of their fierce exchanges at family gatherings took place in Spanish and Yiddish, so they could only intuit each other's insults. But I never heard Granddad curse in English.

Granddad was always nice to me, in his way. When alone with him, I made a special effort to avoid topics that might irritate him. Since neither he nor I excelled at small talk, we both generally looked for activities to occupy our time together.

We listened to baseball games (there was no television in Kansas City until I was in high school) and played lots of gin rummy, with me constantly asking him for advice, whether or not I wanted or needed it. When I got to high school, Granddad introduced me to cigars, allowing us to puff our way through long silences.

* * *

I'm not sure I ever really got to know Granddad. Years later, for Grandma and Granddad's fiftieth wedding anniversary party at Oakwood Country Club, Gary and I were supposed to say something special about them. Grandma stories abounded. But when it came to Granddad, it wasn't easy. Gary described how well Granddad grilled hot dogs. I talked about him and cigars.

* * *

Besides his family—meaning his beloved Ada and those who shared his blood—Granddad had only one great passion: his construction business. He loved reading plans, supervising jobs, and negotiating with subcontractors. He doted on Mom, his office manager; she reciprocated by regularly introducing herself as Florence Hoffman Cortés, an unusual practice in those days. Sometimes she added, "Morris Hoffman's daughter," which infuriated Dad, who viewed this as a conscious rejection of him as part of her identity.

The family master plan called for me to join the business after college. To prepare me, Granddad patiently taught me about construction. The problem was, I was a lousy, disinterested student.

To try to light a spark, Granddad would occasionally assign me to one of his jobs as an unofficial apprentice who was supposed to learn the business from the ground up. I'd spend summer days with different artisans—carpenters, plumbers, painters, or electricians. But whenever I could I would slip off and read, which didn't bother the workers because it relieved them of having to worry about me and my ten thumbs.

During high school summers, Granddad began taking me on day trips to visit out-of-town projects. One was in St. Joseph, about sixty miles north of Kansas City. The job was also right across the street from a public baseball field.

Once, late in the morning, while Granddad was involved in discussions with workers or his client or somebody, I went over to the field and got into a pick-up game. It lasted for hours, until

I spotted Granddad standing alone, watching grimly. When I ran over to him, he tersely informed me that he'd been looking for me everywhere.

During the drive back to Kansas City, I tried several times to start a conversation. Granddad responded succinctly and wearily. He barely said goodbye when we got home.

That was the last time Granddad took me on an out-of-town business trip.

13

Grandma Hoffman

With Mom, Dad, and Granddad now focused on the expanding construction business, Grandma became my special pal. I always felt more at ease with her than with anyone else in the family, including Mom and Dad, who were both unpredictably temperamental. Grandma never seemed to get angry. And she loved to tell stories, many of which turned out to be true.

The Weinsafts, Grandma's family, were classic Jewish storytellers—colorful, funny, outlandish, inventive. This was especially true when you got a room full of them, like when we spent time with Grandma's sister Mary and her brother Joe, a moderately successful life insurance salesman who probably would have done better if he had devoted more time to selling and less time to making people laugh. Weinsaft gatherings were so much livelier than Hoffman ones, which tended to be heavy, serious, and dour, virtually devoid of laughter.

Because I was nearly six years older than my brother, Gary, I did lots of things without him during his early years, like spending weekends at my grandparents' Kansas City home at 3716 Benton Boulevard, or weeks at their Lake Lotawana summer house. Safe and secure in Grandma's living room, I would listen in awe to stories that she had just heard on the radio or, occasionally, that she had read in the newspaper. On long walks around the lake, she would tell me about ghostly creatures that lurked in the surrounding woods. Best of all were her stories about King Arthur and the Knights of the Round Table.

With little formal education, Grandma didn't read all that well. But she loved to buy book series, like The Book of Knowledge and Journeys through Bookland, because they looked so good on the shelf. Fastidious Grandma insisted on always keeping them in correct order, gently admonishing me if I didn't put one back in its proper place.

For some reason, probably because they were so handsome, she bought a set of books on King Arthur, though she had never previously expressed any interest in knighthood. These weren't children's books, but after she haltingly read the first few paragraphs of King Arthur, I was hooked.

From then on, when it came time for Grandma to read to me, I almost always asked for King Arthur. Grandma would try to redirect me to something more age-appropriate (meaning easier for her to read), usually to no avail.

But when Grandma read King Arthur, she spent most of her time looking straight at me, not at the book. Stories of knights and sorcerers and princesses and quests and adventures poured out of her mouth, with lots of expression and the mesmerizing inverted Yiddish syntax that she never lost.

Then I learned to read. For Grandma it was bittersweet when I abruptly announced that now I wanted to read to her. It was as if I had taken away one of her most cherished roles, that of guiding me into distant times and worlds.

When I became old enough to wend my way through the King Arthur books on my own, I was taken aback. The stories were so different from the ones I remember Grandma reading to me. When I mentioned this to her, she thought for a moment and then said she had told me King Arthur stories she had read elsewhere, although she couldn't remember the name of the book.

What I do recall is how much better Grandma's stories of King Arthur's court were than the ones I read in the series, or would ever read in the future.

OUT SOUTH

14

The Park

Grandma helped me escape into fantasy worlds. But she couldn't help me deal with the real challenges of moving into a new neighborhood. Actually, the neighborhood wasn't the biggest problem. I was. Somehow, I had grown up chicken shit, a cowardly crybaby.

I was seven, a second grader, when we moved into our first home on the southwest corner of Rockhill and Oak, in the middle-class, south part of Kansas City. To my delight, our home sat catty-corner from a small public park loaded with swings, parallel bars, a slide, a jungle gym, a small basketball court, and plenty of space to play football and baseball. To my chagrin, the park also turned out to be the arena in which young boys had to undergo their neighborhood initiation rites.

Painfully shy, I asked Mom to take me over to the park to meet the kids during the first weekend in our new home. She took me there and then left me, at which point one of the kids jumped me and beat the hell out of me. Later I learned that all new boys got beaten up until they proved they could stand up for themselves. I couldn't, and ran home crying.

Furious, Mom headed out the door. She'd tell those kids never to pick on her little boy again. Equally furious, Dad told Mom to shut up, sit down, and not turn me into a spectacle.

That same week, Dad bought me my first pair of boxing gloves, put up a punching bag in the basement, and began teaching me how to fight. Dad was built like a square, his shoulders about equal to his height. When he boxed in college, he had relied on his powerful left hook. However, because of my long, skinny arms, he emphasized my left jab as well as my sneaky, if tepid, right hand.

Every night I worked out on the bag, then sparred with Dad. At first it was worse than going to the park. Dad took it easy on me, but I could still feel his left hooks, even when I blocked them. I learned pretty quickly that my best recourse was to jab and move, trying to stay away from that left-hooking maniac.

Slowly, boxing became more natural. I still got beat up regularly at the park, but now I was fighting back. Then came my Sunday afternoon with Carl Robertson, who had built a well-earned reputation as one of the toughest second graders.

That Sunday, Carl decided it was his turn to beat up the crybaby from across the street. The fight must have gone on for hours...or at least ten minutes. Carl hit me, but I hit him, too. We slugged; we wrestled; we spit; we pulled hair; we rolled in the dirt. Mom and Dad watched from our front yard, Mom in tears, Dad stoical.

Finally one of the older kids stepped in and broke it up. Nobody won officially, but after that fight nobody picked on me—not because they were afraid of me, but because I had completed the ritual. By fighting back and holding my own, especially with Carl Robertson, I had become a park member in good standing. Later, Carl and I became pretty good friends.

But Dad kept sparring with me and teaching me new boxing tricks, just in case. Partly it was to toughen me up, not just for the street, but also for life. As we rested after sparring, Dad would talk to me about strategy, including the necessity of avoiding fights if at all possible, and about ethics and values, especially honor and chivalry. He would continue those conversations with me for the rest of his life.

15

J. C. Nichols School

J. C. Nichols Elementary School sat imposingly atop a steep hill, one block south of our home. Compared to the park, Nichols was a cup of tea.

All the kids were white, as Kansas City public schools were racially segregated. I was the only one with a Spanish surname or Mexican ancestry, but I was so fair skinned that it didn't seem to matter. The swarthiest boy in my grade was a big Greek named George Makris who had a beautiful baritone voice. When we were in seventh grade (our last at Nichols), he sang as one of the "We Three Kings" at the Nichols Christmas pageant. Almost all Nichols students were Protestants or Jews. Catholics—there were plenty in our neighborhood—invariably went to parochial school. But religious differences didn't seem to mean much at Nichols. One of my best Jewish friends, Arnold Mandell, also sang as one of the three kings.

I came down with laryngitis the day of the tryouts, but I doubt that I would have been chosen anyway. Still, I was disappointed. So was Mom, the still-aspiring opera singer. I did better playing piano, earning honorable mention in the citywide classical music competition.

Dad took satisfaction in the fact that I could now hold my own at the park, while Mom took pride in my meager musical accomplishments. And they both became active when I joined the Cub Scout pack that met weekly at Nichols.

Just about every Nichols boy joined the Cub Scouts, as they did at most other Kansas City schools. Scouting was Kansas City's thing. In those days, Cub Scouts were ages nine to eleven. Our pack met once a week at Nichols, and every spring we played baseball.

With eighteen dens, our pack was big enough to have its own hardball baseball league. The adult leaders created six teams, each consisting of three dens, and on Sunday afternoons the teams played four-inning games in a five-game round-robin schedule.

I don't remember the first year, but during the second year, when I was ten, we won the league championship. League rules mandated that everyone on the team had to play at least one inning. We had two good pitchers, so the opposition seldom hit the ball out of the infield. Since I was a pretty mediocre athlete, they stuck me out in right field where I could inflict the least damage. I caught a few balls, but mainly I threw hits back to the infield.

The next year, our team stunk. Because I was one of the few eleven-year-olds on the team, Dad, our coach, made me pitch.

For the first game, only seven of our players showed up. League rules permitted short-handed teams to choose fill-in players from other teams if they happened to be there at the time. Several very good players were hanging around, so it was a great opportunity for us to recruit two of them.

But then my little (six-year-old) brother, Gary, and his pal, Bruce Woodring, said they wanted to play. When I urged Dad to choose two good players from other teams, Gary and Bruce started crying, so Dad told them they could play and put them in the outfield.

Truth be told, I was an awful pitcher. I managed to survive the first inning with a 2–1 lead, but in the second inning the other team poured it on. As fly ball after fly ball fell safely in the outfield, with Gary and Bruce unable to catch or even throw the ball all the way back to the infield, runs mounted up. I begged Dad to take me out, but he told me to get the hell back on the mound and finish the inning. I did, finally, after the other team scored nineteen runs.

In the third inning, Dad switched me to catcher and let the catcher pitch. He only gave up five runs before we mercifully made our three outs in the top of the fourth, ending the carnage at 25–5.

I was both humiliated and angry. Publicly humiliated because I had pitched so badly. Privately angry at Dad for playing those two little creeps. I was particularly angry at Gary for contributing to my humiliation, and I could hardly wait to get home and unload on him.

But as we left the field, Gary was all smiles, so proud about playing on his big brother's team. I couldn't unload on him. Dad's honor lessons from our basement boxing sessions had taken root. I was the older brother. Just as it was Dad's obligation to prepare me for the future, it was my obligation to pave the way for little Gary, even if this meant personal sacrifice.

Enough of our players showed up for the rest of the games so that Dad didn't have to choose any more replacements. Our former catcher turned out to be a pretty good pitcher, while I became an okay catcher. We actually won two games, and I didn't have to pitch another inning.

At gatherings of family and friends, Gary often repeated, with pride, the story of how he got to play a game with his big brother. Dad never mentioned the score.

16

Boy Scouts

In April 1946, when I turned twelve, I graduated to the Boy Scouts like just about every other guy at Nichols. I enjoyed it, but eventually it would come to mean even more to Dad. Scouting became essential to his life.

As the years went by, Dad distanced himself from Catholicism, ultimately developing an antipathy to all organized religion. Scouting became a kind of personal faith, helping to fill his religious void. He saw the Scouts as his opportunity to help fill voids in the lives of others, to build better boys, and, thereby, better communities.

Not that Dad's devotion to the Scouts didn't occasionally prove a burden for me. He became adamant about the Boy Scout Oath and Law, expecting Gary and me to follow them to the letter. Above all, we were never to lie when saying something under "Scout's Honor" while giving the Boy Scout sign of three upraised fingers. Unfortunately, being human, I didn't always come through.

One summer, Howard Wayne, Stanley Kleban, and I agreed to meet at Howard's house the next day. But when Stan and I arrived at Howard's house, Howard wasn't there. Understandably miffed at being stood up, Stan and I jimmied open a screen, climbed through the window, got something to eat from the Waynes' refrigerator, left spoons on the sink, and climbed back out. Needless to say, we didn't commit the perfect crime. The Waynes discovered our expert break-in, and for some reason, the shadow of suspicion fell on us. Stan and I predictably denied the accusation. But, with Dad present, Mom went to the court of last resort. "Scout's Honor?" she asked. Caught unprepared, I lied… and felt horrible.

After a sleepless night, I told Mom the truth, figuring she would be more forgiving. She scolded me and then asked me to do precisely what I didn't want to do: tell Dad. I begged her not to make me do that, but she said Dad would understand, that he would be disappointed that I had lied under Scout's Honor, but would be even more disappointed if I didn't tell him.

So I tried...and tried and tried. I don't know how many times I visualized going into Dad's office to tell him, but I finally realized I couldn't. And I didn't. It's the only time I remember blatantly lying to Dad. I know it was the only time that I broke Scout's Honor with him. To this day, I wish I had fessed up. Mom, bless her heart, never asked me if I had.

As you get older, you look back on your life and wish you had done some things differently. It's funny. In my case, most of them aren't big things, at least in the traditional sense, but little things—rash decisions, intemperate actions, and inconsiderate reactions—like lying under Scout's Honor.

If Mom were still alive I'd like to talk to her privately about that incident, although I'm not sure she'd remember it. At the time, Mom had said that she wasn't going to say anything to Dad. I don't know if she did. For Dad's sake, I hope she didn't. I hope he didn't go to his grave having learned, even if it had disappeared from his memory, that his oldest son had betrayed him.

THE HEAVY HAND OF MEXICO

17

Mexico, 1946

In the summer of 1946, shortly after I turned twelve, we took our first long family trip...to Mexico. This had been Dad's dream, a dream that had been gnawing at him: for me and Gary to meet Dad's Mexican family, particularly his mother, who had moved to Mexico City, and Tía Anita, the aunt who had raised him in Guadalajara during the Mexican Revolution.

It was also an opportunity to teach us more about our Mexican heritage. Well, what I really mean is *his* Mexican heritage—not the kind of stuff we saw in Kansas City when Dad would take us over to the Mexican Westside for lunch or some fiesta.

Those trips to the Westside were kind of awkward. Dad loved speaking Spanish, but these weren't his kind of Mexicans. Packinghouse workers, railroad employees, tradesmen, and grocery store owners didn't represent Dad's aristocratic vision of Mexico.

To prepare me for our introduction to *his* Mexico, Dad began what would become a regular pre-trip ritual. He designed a reading plan for me about our destination, so I could more fully understand and appreciate what I would see. (Gary, only six, wasn't part of the ritual.) For this trip, I read books on Mexican history and culture, which we discussed at length, as well as books to intensify our—meaning Dad's and my—use of Spanish. So I was sort of prepared for our five weeks in Dad's Mexico.

From the moment we drove across the border and Dad glee-fully doled out his first small *mordida* (bribe) to a Mexican police officer, he was home. He didn't walk; he strutted. Normally reserved, he became more garrulous, even though his somewhat rusty Spanish didn't measure up to his rich English.

But when we got to Guadalajara, a surprise awaited us: Tía Anita wasn't there to meet us. She had gone off for an extended stay at a spa and left us a note to make ourselves at home in her opulent gated residence.

Tía Anita's absence puzzled me, since she knew we were driving all the way from Kansas City to see her. Dad took it in stride, I thought. Not until several years later did he tell me what lay behind his aunt's absence and how much pain this had caused him.

A passionate Catholic and proud Mexican, Tía Anita had been unhappy when, in 1907, her brother, my grandfather, had returned to Mexico with a Jewish American wife. Since she couldn't have children, she poured herself (and her Catholicism) into her brother's oldest child, my father, especially during those crucial five years after my grandparents fled to the United States in 1913.

Now Dad, too, had married an American Jew. Tía Anita had been dismayed by her brother's marriage, and now viewed Dad's marriage as a personal affront. Dad (and Mom) were welcome in her home, but she refused to receive them in person.

Yet Tía Anita still wanted to see Dad, so she left word that she and her husband, Salvador Gómez, were spending a month at San José Purua, a gorgeous mineral water spa perched on the slopes of a breathtaking canyon. If we wished, we could join her on our way to Mexico City. Dad dutifully accepted Tía Anita's rebuke and cut short our Guadalajara stay in order to spend a couple of days at the spa.

Tía Anita turned out to be a female version of Dad. Same aristocratic bearing, but even haughtier. Same square build. Same measured reserve and authoritative voice. And an even greater sense of imperiousness.

She refused to speak English, even though Dad said she could, thereby shutting Mom and Gary out of the conversation. Since Dad had taught me a modicum of Spanish, I could meagerly participate.

Next stop, Mexico City, for two weeks of spending time with Dad's mother, affectionately known as Mams, and her son, René, a year younger than I. Mams had remarried, to a man some two dozen years her junior, making René my Dad's half-brother and therefore my uncle, despite my age seniority. Mams and her new husband ran a business making boxed lunches for tour groups going to the pyramids at nearby Teotihuacán. Although the work didn't make big bucks, it provided them a small home, and they also sent René to Mexico City's relatively pricey private American School.

Then, with a couple of days left in Mexico City, Dad abruptly announced that we were cutting short our stay to go back to San José Purua. No explanations. And once we got there, he spent most of the time alone with Tía Anita while we swam and clambered around the gorge.

At the time Dad didn't tell us what they talked about. Later I learned that Tía Anita had chastised him for not marrying a Mexican and for not raising Gary and me as Catholics. She insisted on his obligation to pass on his Mexican culture to us. And she was mortified by my choppy Spanish and the fact that Gary didn't speak the language at all.

On the way home, Dad was unusually moody, even hauling off and belting little Gary in our Monterrey hotel room the final night before we crossed the border. (Dad had occasionally used his razor strap on our butts, but this was the first time he had ever slugged Gary or me, except, of course, when we were boxing.)

The Mexico trip had been fun. But it was more than that for Dad, who came back an absolutely new man. Prouder, more assertive, determined—I mean fiercely determined—to raise us Mexican. Since Gary was only six, Dad focused on me. I didn't realize it then, but that trip—especially his long conversations with Tía Anita—had convinced Dad to do battle for my ethnic soul.

18

Dad's Family Burden

Dad's actions quickly revealed how much our trip to Mexico had changed him. But it took much longer for me to grasp the full power that his Mexican family exerted over him.

Dad had admired but feared his tyrannical father. Strong, charismatic, and demanding, my Grandfather Cortés had set standards that Dad tried to meet, but never felt he did. It was as if Dad's father were constantly judging him from the afterlife.

Dad's mother was less imposing physically. A squat, cultured, supremely self-centered woman, Mams could mesmerize with charm even as she demanded dutiful treatment. As her oldest child, Dad felt a special responsibility to Mams, whom he greatly admired and, I'm sure, loved, although this wasn't particularly apparent when they were together. Mams didn't reach out much to her distant children or grandchildren, but over the years I developed a plausible relationship with her, always by my going to Mexico, never the reverse.

I didn't develop a relationship with Tía Anita, who had been such a powerful force in Dad's childhood and whose approval Dad desperately wanted. She died before my next visit to Mexico.

* * *

In the summer of 1963, years after Tía Anita's death, I visited Guadalajara. Her husband, Salvador Gómez, was still living in the family home. I stayed for several days and we had some pleasant but unremarkable conversations.

Then, during my last night there, Salvador brought a friend to supper, a much younger woman who had been Tía Anita's nurse. Salvador acted like a teenager showing off his first puppy love, his manner so unlike the diffident formality he had displayed around his imposing wife. Although he didn't ask me explicitly, I concluded that he wanted me to tell Dad about his girlfriend so Dad wouldn't be surprised when they got married. When I told Dad, he seemed unexpectedly upset.

Dad considered himself the rightful heir to a Mexican something. His father's something had disappeared with the Mexican Revolution, so Dad hoped he would inherit something from Tía Anita, maybe even his old home. Her ire over his marriage to my Jewish mother had put that inheritance in jeopardy. Now it would disappear entirely with Salvador's remarriage.

The issue wasn't the house's monetary value. It was something else. To Dad, Mexico meant Tía Anita and the home in which he was raised. Her death and Salvador's remarriage meant the loss of an important Mexican connection. It was as if Mexico itself had disinherited him.

* * *

After Tía Anita's death, Dad never again returned to Guadalajara. Not to see Salvador, not to visit his old home. Decades later, long after Salvador's death, as Dad lay bedridden, dying from the effects of emphysema, Parkinson's, and dementia, out of nowhere he mused, "I think I'll go down to Guadalajara and visit Salvador. I'd like to see my home again."

19

The Polo Club

The first perplexing evidence of Dad's post-trip metamorphosis was his offhanded announcement, over dinner, that he had joined the Mission Brook Polo Club.

In Mexico City we had gone to several matches of an international polo tournament featuring Mexico's best teams and the Argentine world champions. But Dad had never talked much about horses, nor had I ever seen him on one. So his announcement came as a bit of surprise, although not his manner of announcing.

Being offhanded was Dad's gambit when informing us about his major unilateral decisions. He would toss them out as casually as though mentioning that he had eaten veal steak vesuvio for lunch. That way he could both finesse his arguments and remind Mom who was in charge.

Mom's reactions would indicate whether or not she had been in on the decisions. When upset, she would purse her lips and puff out her cheeks like an adder, while a desperate, cornered-animal look would settle in her eyes. Occasionally she would say something like "You could have at least *discussed* this with me first!" Then she would wipe her mouth with a flourish, slap her napkin down on the table (instead of folding it neatly as was her nearly invariable habit), and retreat into the kitchen or bedroom, slamming the door as she left.

Mom's responses weren't just personal pique. They also reflected the fact that she would have to deal with the financial consequences, since Dad left it up to Mom, a budget-balancing whiz, to figure out how to pay for his arbitrary, fiscally onerous acts. Drawing on the reality of our bank account, Mom sometimes succeeded in talking Dad out of his expensive ventures.

Not this time. You could measure Mom's surprise, anger, and chagrin—as well as her financial worries—by the number of doors and drawers she slammed. The kitchen, bedroom, and even the downstairs bathroom soon resounded with slamming; the polo club announcement drew a twenty-one-slam response.

Dad followed this up by announcing that that "we" were going to the polo game that Sunday...meaning Dad and whoever else wanted to come along. I went. Mom lodged a futile protest by staying home with Gary.

Visions of the posh Mexico City polo club danced in my head as we drove out to Mission Brook, but they quickly vanished as we pulled up to a few barns, a tiny white grandstand with rough, paint-flaking wooden benches for several hundred people, and a small, unadorned cement patio for post-game parties. The stands seldom filled up, polo not being a major Kansas City spectator sport. Mission Brook was no Mexico City.

A few weeks later, again over dinner, Dad casually mentioned that he had bought a polo pony named Cold Stream. Of course, he added, he would eventually need at least two more. Because a polo match was divided into six chuckers (periods) and a pony could be used for only two, a player needed three horses for a full game.

More doors and drawers slammed. Mom was beside herself. Constantly working to keep us afloat financially, she now had to deal with the club membership, polo equipment, and a horse, including boarding and veterinary expenses.

Then there were the twice-a-week afternoon practices, which meant that Dad had to leave the office early. This dragged Grand-dad—who worked morning to night, sometimes seven days a week—into the squabble. Imagine afternoons at the office—Granddad looking vainly for Dad to discuss an urgent business matter and exploding when he learned that Dad had taken off for the polo club.

Sometimes Gary and I went to watch Dad practice, which was terrifying—players galloping up and down the field, mallets swinging every which way, and the hard wooden ball flying at dastardly speeds.

Worse yet, Dad couldn't ride. To swing a polo mallet, he almost always had to slow or stop his horse in order to hit the ball, never swinging in full stride like the real players. Since he could barely control or, for that matter, even stay on his horse, he constantly got in everyone's way. It was only a matter of time before Dad got hurt, maybe badly.

Beyond that concern, his presence on the practice field meant that his team actually had to play three men against four. Before long, players who got stuck with Dad on their team began to show resentment. They never played him in a regular Sunday game.

After a while, Dad began going to practice less frequently and went to fewer games. So it came as no real surprise when one night, over dinner, he quietly mentioned that he had sold Cold Stream, which meant the end of his polo career.

No doors or drawers slammed. We all slept better that night. The three of us didn't have to worry anymore about Dad getting hurt. Mom didn't have to worry about financing Dad's misadventure. And Dad didn't have to worry about making a spectacle of himself on the practice field.

Athletic reality had triumphed over aristocratic fantasies. A possible tragedy had been avoided. But one more safe harbor, into which Dad could escape with his aristocratic Mexican illusions, had been destroyed. I'll never know how much of Dad's dream world disappeared with the sale of Cold Stream. He seldom talked about polo after that.

20

Mams

Dad's polo club affectation turned out to be a transitory distraction, although it did put a dent in our family finances. As always, Mom persevered, managing to squeeze out enough money to cover Dad's brief escapade. However, our second Mexico-related financial challenge was longer lived and became a greater source of family conflict.

I'll make it simple. Every month Dad sent money to Mams. I don't know *when* he started sending it. I don't know *how much* he sent. I don't know *how long* this went on. All I know is that he sent it, and that very fact became a growing source of family tensions.

As the oldest sibling, Dad felt a tremendous sense of responsibility toward his mother. Knowing that she was struggling to make a living with her small business and young son, Dad may have come up with the idea of sending her money.

Or maybe not. Maybe Mams leaned on Dad to start sending money. Regardless of how it started, Mams constantly pressured Dad to increase the monthly amount, and also asked for extra money for special wants and needs. My brother, Gary, ran across some of those pressuring letters in his basement.

I've got a hunch that Dad began sending a little money to Mams before our trip to Mexico, then increased the amount afterward. I infer this from the fact that, by the time of our 1946 visit, Mams was living nicely, albeit modestly, and René was attending private school. Maybe their boxed lunch business was providing that lifestyle, but I doubt it.

I do know that our Mexico trip heightened Dad's sense of obligation to Mams—and also to René, who had become a sort of third son to Dad, his only Mexican-born son. Dad wanted René to have some elite advantages, such as attending private school.

Because our family didn't have much to spare, every time my parents sent a check to Mams, my mother felt a sense of personal loss. It was an irremediable setback in her ongoing efforts to lift her own family up the long ladder from lower to upper middle class.

Mom grew to despise Mams. According to Mom, Mams continually and with increasing imperiousness demanded money from Dad and never expressed any appreciation for the sacrifices that she and Dad (and, indirectly, Gary and I) were making for her.

Grandma and Granddad Hoffman felt the same way. They had worked, saved, and sacrificed all of their lives. Now this Mexican son-in-law was sending *their* money—since Dad worked for Granddad—and their daughter's money and their two grandsons' money to his demanding mother, who looked down on them because their family heritage didn't measure up to hers. Even more infuriating, Dad sent their money to this woman who had forsaken Judaism.

Dad made things worse. When Mom and Dad would argue about the money going to Mams—an increasingly frequent occurrence—Dad would sometimes throw his aristocratic heritage and cultured mother in Mom's face, comparing Mams to my mother's up-from-little folks. Predictably, Mom reported this to Grandma and Granddad.

Mom was becoming fed up with Mams. Dad was becoming fed up with my mother's attitude toward Mams. Grandma and Granddad were becoming fed up with Dad's decisions about Mams. Mams was increasingly becoming a source of conflict.

CAUGHT IN THE MIDDLE

21

Mom and Dad

The polo club affair and Dad's financial assistance to Mams epitomized my folks' marriage. Dad came up with big ideas; Mom was a master of detail. Dad would launch projects; Mom would have to see them through.

Without telling Mom in advance, Dad would invite people over for a party, and Mom would see to it that there was a party when—make that if—the invitees arrived. One year Dad announced during a family dinner on December 30 that he had asked a bunch of friends over for New Year's Eve. Mom busted her butt to get things ready. Two people showed up.

The polo club incident was one of the few times I ever saw Mom at a loss for words. I grew up envying her ability to talk to anyone, seemingly about anything. She passed on that ability to my little brother, Gary, while I followed in Dad's path of restraint in large groups.

In different ways, Mom and Dad were both my pals and my mentors. Both loved to teach. Dad's subjects were history and literature; for Mom it was usually music, especially opera.

Saturday afternoons meant the Metropolitan Opera on the radio. Mom and I would follow along with her opera scores, which she collected fastidiously and lined up alphabetically. Sometimes, particularly during soprano solos, restraint failed and Mom would burst forth into song…loudly. I loved seeing her so happy, but once the music ended she would often turn pensive, maybe thinking of her unfulfilled musical dreams.

With urging from Dad, Mom auditioned for the Kansas City Music Club…and got turned down, with the recommendation that she take lessons and try again. Mom didn't want to; this rejection, like most of her experienced rejections, had cracked her veneer of confidence. But Dad insisted that she begin singing lessons, so she did. A year later she passed her membership audition.

For Dad, just about everything was a teaching opportunity. At the beginning of each summer, he would take me to Kramer's Bookstore to stock up for three months of supervised reading. He liked to focus on one author at a time, so we would wander through the used book stacks until we found a complete series. One year was Hugo, another Dickens, another Cervantes, another Melville. One summer Dad bought a twenty-five-volume set of Alexandre Dumas. Obviously I didn't finish all those volumes, but Dad and I spent three hot, humid months together accompanying d'Artagnan and his fellow musketeers across the decades.

I loved watching Mom and Dad in public. You wouldn't classify them as two of the "beautiful people," but they were striking together. They were only about an inch apart— Mom at five foot seven, Dad at five foot eight—while Mom had trimmed down by more than fifty pounds since her Brunhilde days at Berkeley.

In public, with outgoing Mom breaking the ice and more reserved Dad chiming in with his sly, ironic sense of humor once he felt comfortable, they seemed so at ease among others. But while they could be charming, they also fought—well, more like bickered. Especially when Mom got tired of fixing the loose ends that Dad left in his wake. Or when Dad got tired of Mom completing his statements or irrepressibly correcting his stories.

My wife, Laurel, found Mom and Dad loving but strangely embattled. One of their best friends said they were straight out of *Who's Afraid of Virginia Woolf?* In a perverse way, I found their repartee sort of charming, maybe because each would look at me for approval of some clever line.

Mom and Dad found lots of things to argue about. Ironically, considering their backgrounds, one thing they almost never argued about in front of me and Gary was religion. Religion was a topic for private conversations—one on one—not for groups.

But these private conversations weren't about theology. Rather, they concerned identity and social practice, issues like the faiths of our friends and, as Gary and I grew older, the girls we dated.

Ours was a home of religious conflict only occasionally made explicit through words in public settings, but constantly implicit in frowns and pouts and abrupt departures from the room. Religion was the elephant in the room when it came to family relations, particularly to Dad's relationship to Granddad. And after our trip to Mexico, religion joined ethnicity as a focal point of turmoil when it came to me.

22

Little Carlos

Dad transformed his small study into a Mexican sanctuary. After a long and often frustrating day of wrestling with contracts and negotiations and construction projects and, of course, fighting with Granddad, he would retreat into his study after dinner.

Dad had always had a nice collection of Mexican books and memorabilia. Now, he crammed his study with even more books about Mexico. Night after night he would read and talk to me about the Aztecs, the Conquest, the Revolution, Mexican art and literature...you name it.

And, of course, Dad told me all about our own family heritage, beginning with Uncle Hernán Cortés. Well, maybe. Family lore—some passed on to me by Dad, other stuff from his siblings and their kids, my first cousins—includes various versions of our past. That we are direct descendants (legitimate or illegitimate) of Hernán himself. That we are descendants of his brother. That we are descendants of a cousin who came during or shortly after the 1519–1521 conquest of Mexico.

My late first cousin Gay spent years constructing a family tree, working backward from *her* father's generation (including her father's brother, my Dad). Although the tree revealed how many strands of the Mexican elite flowed down to us, it rendered invisible those other bloodlines that involved servants, mistresses, and one-night stands. Gay ultimately hit a dead end and couldn't be precise about the sixteenth century.

Dad loved talking about our ancestry. It was as if talking about it could transport him out of his Kansas City mundanity. And it was one way he could imbue me with a greater sense of being Mexican.

He also taught me more Spanish. Not just to be able to communicate with me in his native tongue, but also so we could speak privately, even around the others. But Grandma, Granddad, and Mom had also been teaching me Yiddish, the common language of Eastern European Jews and the language of my grandparents' Kansas City courtship.

During family arguments, English would sometimes disappear entirely to be replaced by side-by-side conversations in Spanish and Yiddish, with me the only one who could (somewhat) understand both of them. Imagine our dinner table—me trying to eat dessert while Grandma and Granddad were running Dad down in Yiddish and Dad was blasting them in Spanish.

Maybe more important to family relations, Dad began taking me to Catholic Mass. Occasionally. Alone. Always cautioning me not to tell Mom, who was raising me Jewish. Well, sort of.

I went to Sunday School at B'nai Jehudah, Kansas City's Reform Jewish temple, where Mom, Grandma, and Granddad were members. We celebrated Passover and the Jewish High Holy Days. But we never celebrated Hanukkah, always Christmas, complete with a tree decorated with angels, the three kings, manger animals, and a star of Bethlehem. Even Grandma and Granddad sang "Christ Our Lord" Christmas carols with us. Like many other Reform Jews, they treated Christmas as an all-American event, not a Christian one.

There were no religious symbols in the house. Mom didn't keep kosher or light Friday night candles, nor did Dad push any home religious practices. In fact, for a few years he made an effort to bridge the religious divide by teaching Comparative Religions at the Temple B'nai Jehudah Sunday School.

But after our trip to Mexico, religion became a more contested subject, beginning with the question of what Boy Scout troop I should join. Mom wanted me to join the Jewish troop that met at B'nai Jehudah. Dad insisted on Troop 123, which met at Country Club Congregational Church. Dad won, after a few arguments.

Then the Scouts established the God and Country Award. Since it had Christian overtones, they also initiated the Ner Tamid Award for Jews. When Mom and Dad locked horns over which award I should earn, I settled things by saying I wasn't interested in either, which was baloney.

Yet during our annual two-week summer camp at Boy Scout Camp Osceola, about eighty miles southeast of Kansas City, Dad didn't seem to mind my attending the Sunday morning Jewish service.

You can see why I had so much difficulty determining where Dad had drawn the line between my being Jewish and being *too* Jewish. That is, except when I decided that I wanted a Bar Mitzvah.

23

My Bar Mitzvah

In those days, only the kids who went to Conservative and Orthodox synagogues had Bar Mitzvahs; Temple B'nai Jehudah boys seldom had them. But for some reason, in the fall of 1946, about the time that Dad started taking me to Mass, I decided I wanted one. To this day I'm not sure why. Maybe it was from watching my synagogue friends become the centers of attention at their Bar Mitzvahs and, of course, opening their scads of gifts. Maybe I liked the ritual. Or maybe it had something to do with religious conviction…or confusion.

Mom seemed pleased, but unusually restrained. I suppose I should have become suspicious when she asked me not to tell Dad so that we could surprise him, pleasantly, I assumed. Or when my Hebrew teacher only came to our house when Dad was gone. But I was just twelve, naive, and excited about reading Hebrew in front of the congregation.

Then, one day, while the Hebrew teacher was working with me—in Dad's Mexican study!—Dad came home early. We saw him drive up. Frantic, Mom went out to meet him.

Through the study door I could hear Dad shouting his favorite calumny, "That son of a bitch." I hoped he wasn't referring to me.

Their bedroom door slammed. Mom came in and told the Hebrew teacher he'd have to go. "Why, Mom?" I asked. She just sent me over to the park.

When I came home, Dad was gone. Mom said, in a broken voice, "Junior, your father doesn't want you to have a Bar Mitzvah." This time I didn't ask why.

The allure of a Bar Mitzvah disappeared. In its place lay my fear that I had exacerbated our family's ethno-religious divide.

24

California, 1948

In the summer of 1948, the four of us went to California, our second long family trip and my first West Coast visit since I was a baby. Of course this meant a reprise of my pre-Mexico preparations, months of required reading and long discussions with Dad about California history.

Mexico had brought me revelations about Dad. So did California, but it also revealed a new dimension of Mom.

We spent a month in California. Especially during our two weeks in Berkeley, Mom and Dad seemed transformed. They took us to Tamalpais Road in the Berkeley hills to see the former family home, which my Grandfather Cortés had designed and built while he was dying of cancer. They strolled hand in hand around the Berkeley campus, telling us stories about their early days together. Dad even ran into one of his graduate history professors, who took us to his office and graciously spent time talking to us. My folks' faces reflected the joy of rediscovery, but also wistfulness for an imagined California life that had eluded them.

* * *

Then there was family. Dad, the oldest sibling, was anxious for Gary and me to meet his brothers and sisters. For years he had regaled me with stories of how close they all were. Yet only his brother Vinnie had ever come to Kansas City—for a few days on navy leave during World War II—and Dad had visited California only once since 1934. So I was looking forward to observing the fabled Cortés camaraderie. I didn't see it.

Four of Dad's five siblings lived in California—Alejandro, Eduardo, Vicente, and Susana. The three brothers were friendly, but reserved, like Dad. The most sociable was Ed, casually personable and much easier to get to know than stiff, humorless Alex and laid-back, authoritarian Vinnie.

Most of the family's exuberance ended up in Susie, the pretty, radiant youngest Cortés sibling. Ironically, she had the least reason for joy. Born with severe diabetes, she ultimately became an invalid, and suffered as a human pincushion for medicine-filled hypodermic needles. Yet through it all she remained open, outgoing, and cheerful, exuding optimism and seldom complaining. Dad seemed envious of her innate joyousness.

The siblings, including Dad, did share some Cortés characteristics. All had intelligence, having been raised in a home where their highly cultured parents, my Grandfather and Grandmother Cortés, had immersed them in constant cerebral conversation. They were all of square build—except for trim Alex—with shoulders that didn't slope and necks that seemed the size of other people's waists. All were stubborn. (How often I remember Mom screaming at obstinate Dad, whose face would seamlessly turn impassive, as if revealing his distant Indian roots.) And all were self-centered, expecting the earth and other denizens of the earth, including other Corteses, to revolve around them. Eduardo was the only brother who made much of an effort to reach out to others. For Corteses reaching out was something others were supposed to do.

Add to this the fact that the family was scattered—Dad in Kansas City, Ed and Alex in Northern California, Vinnie and Susie in Southern California, Dad's sister Elena in the then-tiny Mexican fishing village of Puerto Vallarta, and Mams and René in Mexico City. Because they didn't put much effort into communication—they seldom wrote, almost never called, and only occasionally visited each other—the close family I had heard so much about turned out to be more like a loose collection of distant relatives.

One of Dad's favorite growing-up stories was about a time that he returned after several months' absence as a student at the University of Nevada, showing up at home unexpectedly while Mams and her kids were engaged in a heated discussion around the dinner table. Nobody bothered to say hello or even acknowledge his presence. Finally, Mams glanced up, said "Why don't you sit down, Carlos?" and then returned to the argument.

Dad repeated that story as a demonstration of the family's casual closeness. As Dad would say, no matter how long they had been apart, when family members got together they picked up just where they left off, as if they had seen each other fifteen minutes earlier. But that's not what I observed over the years. I think this was Dad's effort—maybe unconscious—to preserve his myth of a close family, despite the virtual absence of communication.

* * *

But California family wasn't just about Dad. It was also about Mom. On that trip I met lots of Mom's uncles, aunts, and cousins, from both the Hoffman and Weinsaft sides. Most important of these relations was Mom's cousin Sylvia Lewis, daughter of Granddad's sister, Mania.

Born in Kansas City, Sylvia was raised a block away from Mom on Benton Boulevard. She had two older sisters, and Mom, who was near Sylvia's age, became like her third sister. For Mom, an only child, this was a blessing.

They played together, spent hours in each other's homes, and went to the same neighborhood school. When as a child Mom lay in bed, nearly dying of scarlet fever, Sylvia sat for hours outside Grandma Hoffman's house and, as she often told me, cried almost nonstop until Mom was out of danger.

Then came Mom's turn to cry. At age twelve, Sylvia left Kansas City. Like many of the other Hoffmans and Weinsafts, her family moved to California. Mom was heartbroken…and alone.

That's one of the reasons she went to college at the University of California, Berkeley—to be near her first cousin, her lost sister. And it was through Sylvia that Mom met Dad.

In the Berkeley hills, the Corteses lived next door to the Lewis family. One of the Lewis brothers, Robert, began dating Sylvia, then Sylvia Rabinowitz. In the fall of 1932, Sylvia and Robert arranged a blind date between his neighbor, Carlos, and her Kansas City cousin, Florence. And so their story began.

By 1948 Bob and Sylvia were married and had four children. They lived in Berkeley, where Bob was a physician. (Four years later they would become my surrogate parents during my 1952–1956 undergraduate years at UC Berkeley.)

For those two weeks in 1948, Mom and Sylvia couldn't get enough of each other and spent almost every day together. In personality, Sylvia was much like Mom—fun, outgoing, and loquacious. They talked for hours, mainly about family, and unlike during our time with the Corteses, silences seldom intruded. I loved listening to the two of them rambling on and on. Gary and I didn't have much to contribute. Even if we had, we probably couldn't have gotten many words in.

I had seldom seen Mom as happy as when she was with Sylvia. Tears streamed down her face when we left for Kansas City.

Like the Mexico trip two years earlier, California was fun, but tainted fun. The trip had exposed to me new dimensions of the importance of family to Mom and Dad. But it had also revealed that for both, family was a painful source of unfulfillment.

THE OUTSIDER

25

Southwest High

California had distracted me from thinking about Kansas City. This included the fact that I was about to begin my freshman year at Southwest High School in the fall of 1948.

Actually, I had already spent the 1947–1948 school year in the massive Southwest High building, although I wasn't officially in high school. Kansas City had just launched eighth grade. Before that, students went directly from seventh grade in elementary school to becoming high school freshmen. Because there were no middle schools or junior high schools, the district wedged eighth graders into already-crowded high school facilities.

My eighth-grade friends and I had just finished an entire year of being elementary school top dogs. Now we found ourselves at huge Southwest High, surrounded by older kids, some by four years. Worse yet, eighth grade girls went for older boys, relegating us to the bottom of the Southwest food chain.

I was very shy. And when I looked into the mirror I saw a skinny, gawky, wimpy-looking nerd with long bony arms and Dumbo ears. On top of that, I've always looked young for my age. Now in my mid-seventies, with relatively few wrinkles and plenty of lightly graying hair, that's a blessing. But at thirteen I wanted hair, dark body hair, above my lip, on my chest…everywhere, especially during communal showers after physical education class.

Well, at least eighth grade had term limits. I was really looking forward to returning the following fall a year older. But I wasn't prepared when discrimination smacked me in the face at the beginning of my freshman year.

Now and then my family talked about bigotry. Dad sometimes angrily shared his personal encounters with people who disliked Mexicans. Sporadically, Mom would mention some slight that she would chalk up to anti-Semitism. Pogroms and anti-Semitism had driven Jewish families like the Hoffmans and the Weinsafts from Europe, the reason why Grandma and Granddad resisted telling us much about the old days. Then there were stories about one relative who served on the crew of the *Exodus,* the ship taking post–World War II Jewish refugees to Palestine, later Israel.

But my family avoided one topic—how discrimination might intrude on my life. Maybe they didn't think about it or feel it was appropriate to talk about. Or maybe they just didn't know how to talk about it.

When it came to racial discrimination in Kansas City, the evidence was everywhere. Kansas City was racially segregated by law—schools, public swimming pools, movie theaters, and even seating at the municipal baseball stadium, where a chain-link fence ran from the top of the grandstand down to the playing field, restricting African Americans to seats far down the right field line.

The city's racial division was primarily black–white. In practice this meant separating Negroes from everybody else. For purposes of legal segregation, Kansas City treated Latinos, Asian

Americans, and Native Americans as honorary white people. Well, maybe off-white.

Religion was more complicated. Kansas City's racial boundaries were embedded in law, but its religious dividing lines were nearly as deeply embedded in custom. Those divisions deepened as kids grew older, particularly when they reached dating age.

At Nichols Elementary School, religious differences didn't seem to mean much, except that Jewish kids took off for Rosh Hashanah and Yom Kippur, earning the envy of our Protestant friends. We played ball together, spent nights at one another's homes, even went Christmas caroling together. After school and on weekends, Nichols kids also hung out with neighborhood Catholics who attended St. Peter's parochial school. We all—Protestants, Catholics, and Jews—enjoyed going together to Church League basketball games, held in the Nichols gymnasium. Country Club Christian and Wornall Road Baptist were just team names to us, not indicators of social divisions or launching pads for theological discussions.

But this neighborhood camaraderie didn't prepare me for the reality of Southwest High. Nor had my folks prepared me. Maybe their own ethnic and religious tensions made this topic too difficult to broach. Or maybe they didn't fully realize what my mixed background would mean in the new teenage social world I was about to enter.

I was still on a high from my California trip when my freshman year started. Yet I quickly took a crash course in what it meant to be a Mexican-Austro-Ukrainian-Belarusian-Catholic-Jew in a world of rigid racial and religious boundaries.

At Southwest, fraternities and sororities were a big deal. No, make that *the* big deal. Belonging or not belonging to a fraternity or sorority essentially determined the dividing line between being an "in" or an "out."

Fraternity and sorority members always wore their pins, the silent, omnipresent public proclamations of who belonged…and who didn't. Clubs had their own tables in the school cafeteria, unofficial but sacrosanct. And Southwest's unwritten social rule was that fraternity boys and sorority girls should generally restrict their dating to club members.

Fraternities and sororities had surrounded us from the time we got to Southwest. But because eighth graders were not eligible for high school activities like sports and literary societies, I assumed that our marginality was just a normal transitory phase.

It was transitory for lots of my old Nichols pals. At the beginning of my freshman year, most of them showed up wearing fraternity pins. I wanted to belong, too. Why had I missed out?

At first I assumed it was because we had been gone for much of the summer, when new members were being chosen. So I began asking about joining a fraternity. That's when I learned the truth. For the first time having both a Jewish mother and a Mexican Catholic father made a real difference. Together this meant social purgatory.

My buddy Arnold Mandell got me invited to his Jewish fraternity's rush party, but I got turned down. Some of Arnold's fraternity brothers had raised the issue, "How could a guy with a Mexican Catholic father be a real Jew?"

When I asked my Christian friends about joining their fraternities, they all gave the same answer. They didn't take Jews. No animosity, just blind adherence to tradition. No Jews Allowed.

I'm not sure I've got the words to capture my full range of emotions—rejection, isolation, anger, antipathy. I mean antipathy against both Christians and Jews. I'd gone to school with them, played ball with them, and spent nights in their homes. But when it came to important stuff, like fraternities and dating, I couldn't escape my folks. My freshman year was awful.

Then Kansas City voters came to my rescue. In the spring of 1949 the Kansas City public schools asked voters for a small tax increase, warning that without it they might have to shorten the next school year. But voters defeated the tax proposal. True to their word, district officials cut the 1949–1950 school year from forty weeks to thirty-four. If this situation continued, Kansas City schools could lose their accreditation, hurting students' college eligibility. (As it turned out, a tax increase passed the following year, permitting schools to resume their full schedule.)

The tax defeat played right into Dad's hands. Ever since returning from Mexico, Dad had been pushing to send me to a private high school like he had attended in California. But Mom, who knew we couldn't afford it, had prevailed, using the harsh logic of our bank account. Now, however, with college in jeopardy, Dad insisted. He suggested Rockhurst, a fine local Catholic school.

Dad's suggestion sent chills up the others' spines—Mom, Grandma, and Granddad. So Mom and Dad reached a compromise. They decided to send me to Pembroke-Country Day, the local private boys' school.

To this day, I don't know how they were able to afford it. Maybe they couldn't. Gary and I have a hunch that Grandma and Granddad may have footed the bill...or at least part of it. After all, the only, unthinkable alternative was seeing me go to a less expensive Catholic school.

26

Pem-Day

At first, tiny Pem-Day seemed like paradise, with small classes and fewer than forty sophomores. This meant I could participate in sports, theater, and other things I would never have tried at huge Southwest. During my sophomore year I made the football and track teams, although I was mediocre at both, and won the Headboy Tablet for earning the highest grades in the entire high school. Best of all, there were no fraternities to make you feel like an outsider.

Pem-Day made a conscious effort to reduce cliques. Students were assigned to specific lunch tables, each under the supervision of a faculty member. Every month brought a seating reassign-ment. This meant that sooner or later you got to (or had to) have lunch with every same-grade classmate and with numerous fac-ulty members.

But day-to-day friendliness didn't translate into nights and weekends. On Mondays, Pem-Day would buzz with sto-ries about parties at so-and-so's house or at some country club, reminding me that I was still an outsider, with social class now added to the mix.

Unlike Nichols and Southwest, where students were middle class, Pem-Day was a school of wealth and country clubs. More-over, country clubs operated on the same social rule—Restricted, meaning No Jews.

There was a Jewish country club, Oakwood, to which Grandma and Granddad belonged. But we couldn't afford it, and that was another place where Dad had drawn the religious line.

We certainly weren't paupers. I just felt like one at Pem-Day. Think about it.

I was neo–middle class in a school of the wealthy. Shy in a school of casual, upper-crust self-confidence. Jewish in a school of Protestants. (Later I learned that Pem-Day strictly limited the number of Catholics and Jews. I wonder if I helped fill both quo-tas.) And, to top it off, I was Mexican.

On the first day of my first class at Pem-Day (only eight stu-dents, as I recall), the teacher called the roll, but didn't mention me. I raised my hand and indicated that me had missed me, Car-los Cortés. Looking at his class list, he announced that he had already read my name, Carl. In front of my new classmates I repeated, several times, that my name was Carlos, not Carl.

Not seeming to appreciate my insistent clarification, the teacher kicked me out of class and sent me down to the headmaster's office. They called my folks and Dad stormed over to school. I was terri-fied he'd be furious at me for getting into trouble on my first day at the new school.

But he wasn't. In fact, he was proud of me for standing up for my name, his name, our Mexican name. Dad lectured the headmaster: "My son's name is Carlos! His father's name is Carlos! His grandfather's name was Carlos! And I'll be damned if you're going to call him anything but Carlos!" After that, they didn't.

Oh, I guess I ought to mention the class where this happened. Spanish.

27

Philmont

Pem-Day was better than Southwest. But having to deal with being an outsider in terms of class and ethnicity, as well as religion? Well, it was too much. I sure was glad when the school year ended.

Better yet, I was really looking forward to a new adventure: a two-week stay at Philmont, the National Boy Scout Ranch nestled in the mountains of northern New Mexico. Little did I know that identity issues would follow me, even to that distant land.

Some forty of us from Kansas City went to Philmont that summer. For two weeks we rode horseback over mountain trails and camped out in glorious forests. It was great...except that I never completely got away from Kansas City.

Even before our chartered bus arrived in Philmont, prior animosities had surfaced, new tensions had developed, and cliques had formed, sort of like gangs. During the day, with adult leaders present, antagonisms remained pretty well under wraps. But nearly every night, after the leaders had gone to sleep, we'd slip out of our tents and begin the serious business of taunts, slurs, and personal challenges.

Race was no issue for us. The Boy Scouts operated with Kansas City–style segregation, so there were no Black kids in our contingent. The major source of identification and contention was your high school, signifying what neighborhood you came from and to what social class you presumably belonged.

There were tough working class boys from the north part of Kansas City. Then there were midtowners from neighborhoods like the one where Mom was raised. But northenders and midtowners both viewed those of us from south Kansas City as spoiled wimps.

And I went to Pembroke-Country Day. It occupied a special place of…well, not exactly honor. We were known derisively as the Pemsy Daisies, the living embodiment of wealth, class arrogance, and country club life.

For me, this was a total piss off. Me, an outsider at Pem-Day, having just spent an entire year envying that kind of life. Now, in the eyes of most of the others at Philmont, I *was* that life.

There was only one other Pemsy Daisy—Pat Daleo, a big, tough, broad-shouldered, olive-skinned Italian American, who played fullback on our football team. Nobody messed with big Pat, so they focused on me. This meant that I, Mr. Pemsy Daisy, had to prove myself with brawn, which I didn't have much of.

But first the northenders and midtowners had to settle a long-standing score. Funny, I still remember the names of the combatants: Chad of the northenders; Vince of the midtowners. A few days after our arrival, the two of them had it out, mano a mano. Chad won by smashing Vince in his…in his most vulnerable spot, leaving him groaning on the ground. The next day the northenders let me know that tonight was my night.

I can't remember what we did that day. My mind was focused on what I had to do that night. I pondered the lessons Dad had taught me in our basement boxing sessions, particularly the importance of dictating the rules of engagement.

So I came up with a simple plan. If the entire north-end crowd jumped me, I was dead meat. My only chance was to bait them into choosing one person to fight me and hope I could hold my own.

After the adult leaders had gone to bed, I went out to face my destiny. When the northenders confronted me, I summoned up false bravado. "Can't handle me one at a time, huh, you gutless creeps!" The gambit worked.

Fortunately, Chad, a truly tough dude, was still basking in the previous night's triumph. So they chose one of the others, a pretty big kid. But I had something else going for me—desperation, which can be a great equalizer.

The moment the kid stepped forward, I hit him with Dad's left jab, once, twice, three times. His nose started bleeding. Now, I had nothing against him, but I knew I had to make a statement to the entire north-end crowd. If I didn't, the rest of my Philmont stay would be hell. So I went crazy and kept on punching. He covered up, then went down. Not exactly a knockdown; I was no George Foreman.

Then, I don't know what got into me. "Okay, who's next? Come on and get yours!" Silence. They were probably stunned that this madman had just discarded his Mr. Pemsy Daisy disguise. Before they could change their minds, I turned my back on them—sort of like a victorious matador—and sauntered over to my tent, trying to hide my terror with my best imitation tough-guy walk.

That was my first, last, and only Philmont fight. I had proven that I was okay, at least for a Pemsy Daisy.

The next day the other kid and I shook hands. His nose had stopped bleeding. My hands were probably more bruised than his face.

But Philmont had hit me with its own punch in the gut. I remember something Graham Greene once wrote: "In every childhood there is always one moment when the door opens and lets the future rush in." Well, Philmont was my moment.

When I joined my folks for a week in Santa Fe, I wasn't about to ruin their vacation by unloading on them. How crappy the last two years had been. To be a Jew lost among the goyim and a Mexican lost among Jews. To be a shy, middle class kid sharing school but not social life with the Protestant country club elite. To have spent two weeks at Philmont representing the Pemsy Daisy world to which I didn't belong. A perennial outsider to just about everybody.

I wanted answers! I just wasn't sure of the questions.

But those conversations would wait until we got home. Then we would talk—and talk seriously—about uncomfortable topics that the family had consciously avoided and resolutely suppressed.

SEARCHING FOR SELF

28

Conversations from Hell

When I got back to Kansas City, I began talking to my family. I mean *really* talking to them. Not just talking, but prying, burrowing, pushing, probing, challenging.

Of course I knew there were family tensions. I'd seen them, the silent glares at the dinner table, the angry reactions to Mams, the disagreements over my Boy Scout awards, and the blow-up over my Bar Mitzvah. But for the most part the family had made a real effort to hide the depth of their animosities and the breadth of family chasms from Gary and me. Now I was trying to break down their collective wall of protective silence.

And I did, slowly but surely, mainly through relentless one-on-one conversations with Mom, Dad, Grandma, and Granddad. All four provided special takes on the family troubles, why they had developed, and who was most at fault. And they all urged me not to share their stories with Gary. He was too young. It was big brother's duty to protect him.

At the core of their troubles were the differences in their backgrounds, differences that had poisoned their relationships from the beginning. Dad had little in common with my grandparents. But they had lots that separated them—culture, class, religion, education, and ethnic identity, for starters. These issues lent an irresolvable subtext to the business and to every family gathering.

When Dad's family fled from Mexico, they lost most of their wealth. Yet Dad was raised with a deep sense of class, a sense he never lost. Granddad Hoffman had to struggle for each step up the socioeconomic ladder. Although he made money, he never acquired Dad's inherent sense of class. A sense of power, yes, but never class. Nor did he seem to try. Granddad was too basic for that.

That unbreachable class divide loomed large, particularly when nourished by ethnic, religious, and educational differences. And their mutual recognition of that divide made it even more poisonous.

On top of that, Dad and Granddad were now in business together—in Granddad's business, to which he had devoted half of his life, building the company slowly, arduously, sometimes painfully. His creation, his kingdom, his identity, his very being. Dad's becoming part of Granddad's business had helped us financially, but it had exacerbated personal tensions by forcing the two of them into constant, suffocating contact.

Moreover, Dad and Granddad looked down on each other and, worse yet, both of them knew it. Dad looked down on Granddad because of his lack of culture and education. Granddad looked down on Dad because of his aristocratic bearing and Granddad's belief that Dad couldn't have made it on his own despite his education.

Then came their personalities. Both were stubborn as hell with explosive tempers, but different, reflecting their basic natures. Granddad was direct, no-nonsense, a man of relatively few words, most of them blunt. Dad was more articulate but also reserved, even sensitive, seething in silence until he blew up, usually away from Granddad, who seemed to intimidate him face to face. (Later

Mom told me that Dad had admitted to their marriage counselor that he saw in Granddad shades of his own father, by whom he had also felt intimidated.)

They all privately told me stories. Many had to do with what it was like being in business together. Others dealt with religion. Not theology or faith, but religion as central to life—socializing, dating, marriage, and children, as well as a sense of belonging or, in my case, a sense of exclusion.

Granddad put it to me straight, in simple, unadorned English that sounded even more severe because of his stern tone and deep, Slavic accent. Granddad saw himself as Dad's benefactor, but his generosity was unappreciated. He had given Dad a chance to make something of himself by taking him into his company, teaching him the construction business, and enabling him to earn good money. Yet Dad had shown little gratitude or willingness to make a real effort to help the company become an even greater success.

Grandma confirmed Granddad's story, but with added Weinsaftian flourishes. She and Granddad had always treated Dad like their own flesh and blood, which was baloney. And she fumed because Dad was sending so much money, money earned because of Granddad, to his ungrateful mother in Mexico City so that she could lead a life of pretensions. To my penny-saving, sock-darning, sheet-mending Grandmother, this was almost sacrilegious.

Dad, of course, saw things differently. He had wanted to be a historian, to teach, and to write books. But he had given up his dreams for our family and to help Granddad with the company. He detested the construction business, being constantly embarrassed by Granddad, who would countermand his instructions without even talking to him, and would tell Dad, over and over, that he never would have made it financially without his help. On top of that, Dad knew damn well that neither Grandma nor Granddad had ever accepted him as a Mexican or as a Catholic.

Mom may have had the saddest story of all. Mom, the seemingly tireless one. Mom, the family rock upon whom everyone relied and from whom everyone demanded. Wife, daughter, and mother. Officially the company office manager. Unofficially, the one in charge of making sure that all of the i's were dotted and t's were crossed, a strong suit of neither Granddad nor Dad. Mom, loved and adored by these two stubborn, demanding, take-no-prisoners men.

Whenever Dad and Granddad had a serious disagreement, which happened often, Mom couldn't win. In fact, she had to lose. They constantly bitched to her, and if she supported one of them, she'd catch hell from the other. If she tried to find a middle ground between these two relentless warriors, she'd hear it from both of them for being disloyal.

It was a delicate situation that called for a conflict resolution specialist. Opinionated Mom, however, lacked that delicate touch. Though garrulous, entertaining, and fun to talk to, she could also be rigid and prickly.

Had Mom been more flexible, she might have been a more successful mediator. But although she had inherited Grandma's innate intelligence, outgoing nature, and charm (to a degree), she had developed few of her mother's subtleties and little of her disarming Weinsaft humor. Particularly in tense situations, the Hoffman side of her personality took over, making her a female version of hard-edged Granddad. Her attempts at working out compromises often ended in her becoming an irritant.

Through conversation after conversation with my parents and grandparents, I unearthed long-hidden family tensions. But, unwittingly, I was also contributing to them. In particular, I had begun to date.

29

Dating

When it came to dating in 1940s Kansas City, Protestants, Catholics, and Jews stuck to their own kind. Peer pressure worked; parents closely monitored religious boundaries.

Once I reached dating age, my family drew religious lines in the sand. Mom bluntly, and Grandma more gently, but just as firmly, told me I should not date Gentiles. My repeated reminders that Mom had married a Catholic drew the inevitable but unconvincing response that, because of his mother, Dad was really Jewish. So what if he had been raised as a Catholic?

Dad didn't expressly forbid me from dating Jewish girls (after all, he had married one). But he made his strong preference clear—I should date Gentiles.

In practice, this meant that I couldn't please both of them. No matter whom I went out with, either Mom or Dad would feel betrayed. Usually this meant silence, sulking, sometimes thinly veiled anger.

Because I had been rejected by both Protestants and Jews, by default most of my social life involved neighborhood Catholics who went to St. Peter's Elementary School or Bishop Hogan High School. Catholic kids seemed less judgmental. Maybe my light skin and Spanish surname helped, especially with their parents; I looked white and sounded Catholic. So it shouldn't come as much of a surprise that my first steady girlfriend, Ann Clark, was Catholic.

Ann and I started going steady early in my junior year. When I told my folks, Mom was furious. Dad seemed more quietly smug than outwardly elated, silently gloating about this victory over the Hoffmans.

Yet I never asked my folks if I could bring Ann home to meet them. And they never offered. Sure, I could have asked. It would have been fine with Dad. But it would have been rubbing salt into Mom's wounds, and she didn't deserve that. Moreover, such an action might have further threatened my family's delicate balance.

Making the situation doubly awkward was the fact that from our home we could see Ann's house, two blocks away on the other side of the wide-open park. Sometimes Ann would be in plain sight (and, of course, Ann could see us). Yet in our year together Ann never met my folks. Not once.

I tried to explain the complications to Ann. Can't say that I was very successful or that she was happy with the situation. But she went along with it until we broke up after my junior year.

30

The Fraternity

Ann was swell. She helped me get through my junior year. But there was something missing. My Catholic friends were great, but I wasn't really part of their Hogan High cohort. So I did something that even today I can't fully explain.

One of my Jewish buddies, Arnold Mandell, had spent his sophomore year in Sarasota, Florida. In the fall of 1950, about the time I started dating Ann, he returned to Southwest. Still chagrined about my earlier rejection by his fraternity, he asked me to rush again. I agreed and was invited to join. Mom was elated. Need I say that I didn't ask Dad for his approval?

I'm still not sure why I said yes to Arnold. Was I awkwardly trying to ease home tensions by balancing Ann with a Jewish fraternity? Or maybe I was still looking for full peer acceptance by some group to buffer my outsiderness at Pem-Day. Whatever the reason, when the fraternity asked me to pledge, I did.

So here I was. A Pem-Day junior pledging a fraternity along with a group of Southwest High freshmen. A boy with a Jewish mother going steady with a Catholic girl. A boy with a Mexican American Catholic father and Reform Jewish mother in a Conservative Jewish fraternity (most of its members, like Arnold, went to Beth Shalom, the Conservative Jewish synagogue). A nerd experiencing his first serious puppy love. A devoted son realizing that he had become, maybe long had been, a major source of family conflict.

I imagine that contemporary psycho-babblers would say I had identity problems. I also imagine they'd be right, although we didn't talk much about identity in those days.

So I carried out my pledge duties. This also meant splitting my evenings and weekends between hanging out with my Jewish fraternity brothers and seeing my Catholic girlfriend, since the twain could never meet.

Then came the frat's spring party, the ultimate test to demonstrate social acceptability before the final vote on whether you had earned the right to become a full member. I wanted to take—should have taken—Ann Clark. So I asked Arnold, who told me flatly that I couldn't. If I did, I might prove what some of the other brothers had suspected...that I wasn't a real Jew.

So I took my second cousin, Ann Hoffman, to the party. The two Anns—Clark and Hoffman—lived next door to each other and were friends. Ann Hoffman also had a steady boyfriend, who trusted us; after all, we were second cousins. So with the mutual consent of both of our steadies, I took Cousin Ann to the party.

With that act, I passed final muster. The fraternity voted me in and I was initiated. But the party experience also taught me a lesson. The fraternity wasn't the place for me.

Initiation had left me feeling empty. It made me realize that simply belonging to a group means nothing, unless it *really* means something. In this case, it didn't. During my senior year I became inactive, not just in the fraternity, but in Judaism itself.

By my senior year, I was just trying to get through high school so I could move on with the rest of my life. And I grew to accept my home situation. But I wasn't fully aware of what my dating and relentless probing had done to my family.

31

Dividing the Spoils

Mom and Dad's marriage had involved a series of contentious compromises. But this new one, precipitated by my dating and my post-Philmont intrusion into family secrets, may have been their most bizarre.

Maybe I should have intuited something from the abrupt change in their personalities during my senior year. Normally reserved, Dad now opened up. He seemed desperate to tell me things that had been bottled up inside of him, to toughen me up, to prepare me for the future.

He poured himself into me—his experiences, his frustrations, his fears, his warnings. How lonely it had been living so far away from his mother in Mexico and his California siblings, whom he seldom saw. How tough it had been dealing with so many people who disliked Mexicans. How I'd have to learn to live on life's margins: a Mexican in a black–white world; so light-skinned that I might not be accepted as Mexican; too Jewish to be fully accepted in Christian circles; and with too much Catholic heritage to be considered truly Jewish.

He insisted that I get away from Kansas City. Away from the suffocating midwestern environment. Away from Kansas City's racial and religious bigotry. Away from the relentlessness of being involved in the family business.

So I made a crucial decision: to leave Kansas City for good. This meant turning my back on the family master plan that I would join Granddad's business after college. It also meant giving up a sure life of security, comfort, maybe even wealth.

But while reserved Dad opened up, outspoken Mom retreated into the background. She began pulling her punches, and almost stopped talking to me about religion, even dating.

Not until years later did I learn the secret behind this sudden reversal of personalities. Once my fierce questioning had exposed our family's delicate balance, the depth of its tensions, and the intricacy of its conflicts, my folks had determined to try to remove Gary and me from the family battlefield.

They decided to divide the spoils, meaning the two of us. Dad would become my primary mentor; Mom would be Gary's. Dad would continue raising me as Mexican (although he had given up his short-lived Catholic renaissance). Mom would continue emphasizing Gary's Jewishness (although Gary says she didn't turn out to be much of a religious mentor, particularly after she began to encounter her own religious tribulations). And neither would challenge the other's supremacy within their agreed-upon domains. It was as if they had settled for a draw: one for her, one for him.

Not that these were rigid side-by-side monopolies. Dad still coached Gary's baseball team. As with me, he was deeply involved with Gary in scouting, Dad's personal religion. And Mom and I were still pals and did things together, like continuing to listen to Saturday afternoon Metropolitan Opera radio broadcasts. (A few years later, while a graduate student at Columbia University, I sold libretti two nights a week at the Met, earning the right to watch the opera from the fourth balcony once the overture had begun.)

But my folks now knew their agreed-upon boundaries—when to take the lead and when to defer. They felt this arrangement was not only best for Gary and me, but also maybe the only way to keep their marriage from collapsing.

There was one other factor. I think they both had grown weary of the religious struggle. Neither had the energy to continue waging war over the two of us, and they hoped that this agreement would allow them—and us—to move on with the rest of our lives.

However, Gary and I knew nothing about their decision. It would be years until we learned about it.

And, as time would show, my folks' agreement proved only a temporary respite before an ever-more-imminent family explosion.

32

Off to College

Mom and Dad's uncharacteristic behavior probably helped me get through my senior year. Home tensions receded, and my final year at Pem-Day actually turned out to be pretty enjoyable. I still went out mainly with Catholic girls, including two semi-serious relationships, but Mom no longer pouted, at least not in front of me. I excelled at school, earning co-valedictorian honors and even being chosen by the other seniors to be the class speaker at the graduation dinner.

And I was learning. I was becoming so adept at maneuvering through social minefields by—how should I put it?—by carefully selecting which parts of my background I would share with prospective dates...and especially their parents. You might say I survived by turning the telling of half-truths into a personal art form.

1952 brought a summer of new beginnings. I had graduated from high school. Gary was preparing to enter Pem-Day as an eighth grader. We moved into Mom and Dad's personally designed, lovingly constructed, L-shaped California ranch–style dream house near the corner of 67th and Belinder in Shawnee-Mission, Kansas, four blocks over the state line. If Dad couldn't get back to California, he was determined to bring California to Kansas City.

And I was planning my Kansas City getaway.

One thing my folks never argued about, even during the worst of times, was where I should go to college. I would follow in their Berkeley footsteps at the University of California (Cal).

When I drove out to California in the fall of 1952, Dad went with me to make certain I got started the right way, meaning the non-Jewish way. At Cal, Dad had belonged to Bachelordon, a local fraternity that had become part of national Alpha Chi Rho. He hoped I would join, too.

Since I was now part of Dad's fiefdom, Mom didn't object, although she skirted the border by privately suggesting that I might at least visit some Jewish fraternities. Well, at least the words came out of her mouth, but I knew that she knew I probably wouldn't. And once she said to me, alone, "You know, Junior, it wouldn't hurt if you dated a Jewish girl now and then!"

Before I went out to the car to head to California with Dad, Mom gave me an enormous hug. I thought she'd never let go.

STRUGGLING TOWARD ADULTHOOD

33

Cal

At Cal, I rushed several fraternities, none of them Jewish. But I ended up joining Dad's.

It was a miracle. Berkeley brought me my first real sense of belonging. Almost overnight I became more confident and outgoing. I dove into activities on this 18,000-student campus like I'd never done at 160-student Pem-Day. I became involved in student publications, ultimately becoming editor of the *Blue and Gold*, the Cal yearbook, and chair of the Student Publications Board during my senior year. I made Phi Beta Kappa. As a sophomore I won the Cal middleweight boxing championship. Best of all, I could now date anyone I wanted without having to walk the parental gauntlet.

Despite Dad's warnings, being Mexican didn't seem to mean much, at least during those undergraduate years. But Judaism still hung precariously over my head, the fear that my mother's stigma might suddenly, somehow, disrupt my new life. So I hid my Jewish past. Not a word about it to anyone on campus.

I enjoyed visiting my myriad California relatives—Corteses, Weinsafts, and Hoffmans. Sylvia Lewis, Mom's sisterly first cousin, and her husband, Bob, were special, becoming sort of my surrogate parents. They lived only about ten minutes from campus, so I regularly hopped over to see them, having long, relaxing conversations about the family with gregarious Syl and briefer exchanges of jokes with Bob, a superb raconteur.

But I shared little about Mom's family with my fraternity brothers. My Jewish heritage remained firmly in the closet.

Once I nearly got outed. You might say I nearly outed myself, because of Gilbert Klapper, a former friend from Southwest High and Temple B'nai Jehudah who was attending nearby Stanford.

Failing to consider the potential ramifications, I mindlessly invited Gil to come up and spend a weekend at my fraternity house. But once we started reminiscing, I realized my blunder. Jewish surnames poured out of his mouth—Stein, Vile, Bernstein, Puritz, Chernikoff, Birinbaum—sometimes around my fraternity brothers.

Now recognizing the peril, I steered conversations away from Kansas City, except when Gil and I went out, which was as often as I could come up with a reason. In the frat house I shadowed him, ready to jump in and change the subject if he ventured anywhere near mentioning my Jewish background or our days together at B'nai Jehudah.

With profound relief I said goodbye to Gil on Sunday afternoon, figuring I had dodged a real bullet. But after Gil left, Peter Norton, a paleontology graduate student, asked me privately if, by chance, I had any Jewish blood.

Now, if there were anyone I should have trusted it was Pete, my mentor and a great pal. But I panicked and lied. I think he could tell, but he didn't say anything.

My new Berkeley self-confidence rode along with me when I drove back that summer to Kansas City, where I had a job as a cable splicer in an automotive supply factory. Shortly after I got home, I met and soon started going steady with a snazzy high school senior named Joanne Staton. Outgoing, Protestant, upper middle class, a card-carrying member of the country club set, and one of the top junior golfers in Kansas City, she was precisely the kind of girl who would have terrified me a year earlier.

Then something strange happened. I had just spent an entire year hiding my Jewish background, but one evening I found myself telling Joanne that my mother was Jewish. And I told my folks—not asked them—that I wanted to bring Joanne home to meet them.

Dad, of course, agreed. After all, this meant another notch on his gun. And Mom treated Joanne with what seemed like genuine cordiality.

When I returned to Berkeley in fall of 1953, for the beginning of my sophomore year, I didn't walk into the fraternity house screaming, "My mother's Jewish!" But I did tell Pete Norton. And when opportune moments arose, I casually mentioned it to other fraternity brothers. And the sky didn't fall. This might have been my first major step toward adulthood.

Then, early in the spring of 1954, I met Pauline Perati.

34

Pauline

I know it's a cliché to say that I fell in love with a girl the first time I saw her. This wasn't quite the case with Pauline, but it sure came close.

One morning in February 1954, as I sat half-attentive in a sociology lecture, I looked across the small horseshoe-shaped auditorium and spotted Pauline. Rather, I saw a stunning face that I had to know. But how? My Kansas City shyness returned with a vengeance.

For the next class meeting I showed up early and stood around until Pauline walked in wearing white bucks, white socks, and a pastel sweater that made her face glow. Once she sat down, I casually sauntered over and took a seat next to her as if it were the last spot in the half-empty auditorium. About two-thirds of the way through the lecture, I managed to ask her some inane question about what the professor had just said, drawing a brief but polite answer. When the lecture ended, I smiled, thanked her for the help, and offhandedly mentioned that I might see her the following week.

I showed up early for the next class and sat near the door at the back of the banked auditorium, just in case. A few minutes into the lecture, Pauline walked in and looked around for a seat. Catching her eye, I motioned to the one next to me. She smiled, came over, and thanked me.

When class ended, I asked her if she wanted to copy my notes for the part of the lecture she had missed. When she said yes, I suggested we do it over a pizza, which led to my asking her to go to a movie.

After that, Pauline and I sat together during every class and regularly went out for lunch. It didn't take long for us to progress from dating to going steady to spending every possible moment together. Just before I headed home for Kansas City that summer, we decided to get engaged.

Like me, Pauline was a sophomore. Also like me, she was shy, but she had such a glorious face, radiant smile, flashing eyes, trim figure, and fetching manner that her diffidence didn't hamper her social life.

I was so smitten that I didn't notice the little things that were really big things that would ultimately undermine us. Let's just call them incompatibilities. Looking back, they were all too obvious; looking into her eyes rendered them invisible.

Then, of course, there was the really important stuff, like the big R—Religion. An Italian American and good Catholic, Pauline regularly attended Mass, took communion, and went to confession. Yet she didn't seem to mind my Jewish background and, of course, was delighted about Dad. Although she didn't pressure me to convert, she insisted on getting married in the Church and raising the kids Catholic, which was fine with me. Except that I had to figure out how I was going to explain all of this to my family.

Just before I headed home for the summer, there came an early June phone call from Kansas City. I could hardly recognize Mom's voice, which cracked as she told me that she and Dad were splitting up.

Driving alone back to Kansas City was horrible, my mind and heart operating on overload. The ache of not seeing Pauline for three months accentuated the pain of thinking about my folks' shattered marriage.

I drove for twenty-four hours, caught a few fitful hours of sleep in Cheyenne, Wyoming, and then, going on adrenaline, drove all night and the next day to Kansas City. When I got home in the late afternoon I found Mom alone. She burst into tears. The summer of 1954 had begun.

35

Summer of '54

Mom and I talked throughout the afternoon and late into the evening. At first I said little, because Mom needed me to listen as she rambled, cried, screamed, and cursed.

We started talking about Dad. Before the night had ended I was telling her about Pauline.

I'm not sure why I told her then. Maybe it was fatigue from the nearly nonstop cross-country drive. Maybe it was our hours of smoking and guzzling Scotch. Or maybe it was just a rash decision, my way of getting it over with, quick and dirty.

Driving across the country, I had pondered how to gently break the Pauline situation to my folks, particularly given their marital turmoil. I had practiced different scenarios, approaches, and explanations, all bad.

But round about midnight, in the semidarkness of our enclosed porch, engulfed by talk, booze, and tobacco, between Mom's screams and tears, I blurted it out. I had fallen in love. Her name was Pauline Perati. She was Catholic and Italian. We were going to get married. Meet Mr. Sensitivity.

In retrospect, I don't know if I could have done it any better... or any worse. There was no way my announcement was going to be well received. It wasn't by anyone except Dad, who delighted in this climactic victory in his struggle for my ethnic and religious soul.

The next morning I woke up with a terrible hangover and, over the next few days, began to assemble the facts. Dad was having an affair. He had rented a small apartment about thirty minutes from our house. He had left the business and had enrolled in the teacher education program at the University of Kansas City.

But beyond the facts, there were wildly conflicting perspectives. I quickly resumed my family role as listener to everybody's stories. Both Mom and Dad viewed me as the only person they could confide in. Dad relied on me because he didn't have anyone else in the family to talk to. Mom relied on me because there were things she couldn't share with Grandma and Granddad. Only fourteen, Gary was still too young to burden.

Summer quickly turned into hell, then went straight down from there. I was working full time. I was trying to make sense of our family crisis. And I had to deal with an unexpectedly turbulent long-distance relationship with Pauline. Here was my typical Monday-through-Friday schedule.

I'd get up at about six a.m. to dress, eat, talk briefly with Mom, and drive forty-five minutes to the steamy Whitaker Cable factory in North Kansas City, where for eight hours I wrapped automotive cables around huge spools for shipment to car manufacturers. I'd get home around six p.m. in time to collapse on the bed for an hour's sweat-bathed nap. (My folks had neglected—or maybe couldn't afford—to install air conditioning in their new dream house, and Kansas City was experiencing an unusually hot, humid summer.)

After showering I would have dinner with Mom and Gary. Then, around eight, I would drive over to Dad's apartment for an hour or so with him, returning home between ten and eleven to a waiting, drinking, strung-out Mom, who would want to talk more about Dad. I usually didn't get to bed until after midnight, hoping that my mind would slow down so I could get some sleep. By Friday night I was a total wreck.

Weekends meant more Mom and Dad—plus time with Grandma and Granddad, who didn't talk only about Mom and Dad, though the subject was never far from the surface. I tried to use weekends to catch up on sleep, while facing the spectre of the upcoming five-day marathon. The rare quiet times were devoted to trying to make sense of everyone's cascading, conflicting stories.

Mom's story: Dad was an ungrateful son of a bitch who looked down on her folks and never appreciated what they—particularly Granddad—had done for him. This would-be aristocrat considered them peons, refusing to recognize that those peons had made it possible for him to send money to support his self-centered mother in Mexico. Now he had been exposed as a philanderer, too.

Dad's story: Mom's family had treated him like shit. He had busted his butt to give her a good life, had answered Granddad's call for help during World War II, and had received no respect for these sacrifices. He hated the construction business and detested working for my overbearing grandfather, staying only to please Mom and to provide a better life for his family. What's more, Mom loved her Daddy more than she loved him. She introduced herself publicly as "Florence Hoffman Cortés, Morris Hoffman's daughter." She stuck up for her father whenever Dad complained about his domineering ways. Beyond that, he couldn't confide in her because she would always run and tell Daddy.

Grandma's story: Grandma was the most upset I had ever seen her. Usually the epitome of composure, she permitted her veneer to crack during the summer of '54. Grandma unloaded her anger on Dad much more than Granddad did. They had welcomed Dad into the family like a son, and this was how he had repaid them. He had treated them like dirt because they didn't come from his kind of sophisticated background. He put on aristocratic airs, even though he owed them his financial success. He talked about his mother as if she were some sort of queen, although she never did anything to help him and never showed him love. More than ever I realized how much Grandma detested Mams.

Granddad's story: As usual, Granddad didn't say much. He was angry about the way Dad had treated his daughter. He had given Dad a great opportunity by bringing him into the company, teaching him the construction business, and paying him a good salary. He had always treated Dad well, yet Dad seemed to resent him, refusing to accept suggestions for improvement. Granddad didn't know what more he could have done.

Years later, my folks' closest friend, Carline Lewis, told me a surprising story about a Dad-less family dinner after I had returned to school that fall. Mom and Grandma had been attacking Dad with increasing fury, when Granddad suddenly blurted out that they should stop criticizing Carlos because sooner or later he would probably return home and rejoin the company. The attacks stopped, at least for that night.

Gary's story: Gary seldom participated in serious family conversations, both because he didn't want to and because the rest of the family felt he wasn't old enough to handle them. Moreover, as Gary shared with me much later, during that last year before the separation, while I was in Berkeley, the verbal clashes between Mom and Dad had escalated in frequency and virulence. This included arguments over the sending of money to Mams, particularly with me in college and Gary at Pem-Day. And, although I can't walk a mile in his moccasins, maybe Gary was more person-ally hurt by Dad's actions. Only once during the entire summer did he go with me to Dad's apartment.

Carlos's story: That summer was a rapid descent into the abyss. Almost every conversation—no matter with whom—was like get-ting kicked in the balls. Afterward I would retreat to my room with nobody to talk to, even as these people I loved were crushing me with a torrent of revelations and accusations. I couldn't discuss things with Gary because he had distanced himself from the fray and was off almost every night with his friends. And I couldn't even find solace in the arms of the girl I loved because she was nearly half a country away.

Solace, hell! Pauline had become part of the problem. Going through her own personal traumas, she began unloading on me, long-distance. She was lonely. She was feeling insecure. I wasn't writing enough. I tried to explain that I was hanging on by a thread, but she cried out for more letters, longer letters, assuring letters.

On top of that, now that Dad's departure had destroyed Mom and Dad's secret ethno-religious compromise, Mom, Grandma, or Granddad would suddenly switch from talking about Dad to coming down on me about Pauline. She was Catholic. She was Italian. How could I get married in a Catholic church? How could I not raise my kids Jewish? Didn't I realize from our fam-ily's experience that religious intermarriage doesn't work? How could I turn my back on them? I was as ungrateful as my father. I was just like my father.

Finally it all became too much. I was halfway to work one morning in mid-August when I suddenly couldn't control the steering wheel. I pulled over and sat for I don't know how long. Instead of going on to work, I drove home.

God bless Mom. She realized that it was her turn to show strength, that I had given all I could, that I couldn't take any more. She took me in to see the psychologist who had been working with her. I spent an hour burying him with two months' worth of pent-up agony. It helped.

The next day I went back to work. Family conversations continued, but differently, with less intensity, with no references to Pauline and with fewer family revelations. Mom and I talked more like the pals we had always been. Grandma eased off, while Granddad continued to show the most restraint. Dad and I mainly exchanged small talk. For all of us, sadness and anger had begun sharing time with emotional exhaustion.

Nobody raised much of a fuss when Dad decided to drive back to California with me so he could meet Pauline. It was an odd drive. Dad didn't talk much about his return to school, his girlfriend, or his future plans. I could tell that things weren't really working out for him, although he never said so.

We spent a nice week together in Berkeley. He liked Pauline, or at least said he did. I'll never know if he really liked her or whether he just liked the idea of a Catholic girl. By the time Dad flew back to Kansas City, I had resigned myself to my parents' divorce.

36

Reconciliation

It was early November when the call came in to the fraternity house. Mom spoke very quietly. "Carlos, I've got a serious question to ask you. What would you think if your Dad and I got back together?"

When I told her that nothing would make me happier, she said that Dad was on the line. Dad spoke up and confirmed that, in fact, they were back together. I'm not exactly sure how or why it happened, since I heard so many versions from different family members. But first let me give my interpretation.

Dad was the key. He hadn't realized how dependent he had become on the construction business for the material good life. After a while, the walls of his modest two-room apartment had probably closed in on him, invoking nostalgia for the huge, rambling, ranch-style dream house that he had designed and built two years earlier.

And for a future with another woman? She may have provided moments of escape and solace, but the idea of a long life together probably—and quickly—proved to be a disappointment to both of them. I think this reality had already begun to set in when we drove back to California, which explains why Dad had said so little about her.

But I think the main factor was that Dad missed having a family. I think he learned that freedom is sometimes better in the abstract than in reality.

Dad's liberation from the Hoffmans had also brought isolation from the woman with whom he had shared more than twenty years of his life. I don't think he had recognized—and still wouldn't openly admit—how much the Hoffman-Weinsaft clan had become his real family. His mother, brothers, and sisters were geographically distant, not family in an immediate, ongoing, meaningful way. (A psychiatrist later unearthed Dad's lifelong pain of being left behind in Mexico in 1913 when his family fled to the United States.)

After Dad's return from California, while he and Mom were still separated, he would drive over to Pem-Day for Gary's football practice. But he didn't sit in the stands like other parents. He sat in his car, where Gary couldn't see him, watching his son block, tackle, and run.

Gary's football practices may have convinced Dad that he couldn't surrender those precious years of family life, as aggravating as they might be. So Dad made his choice for Mom, for the family, for a materially abundant life with the Hoffmans, and for a career he claimed he detested.

But how did reconciliation come about? Dad courted Mom all over again. He called her up for a date and sent her flowers. Never a consistently thoughtful man, Dad knew how to turn on the charm on occasion. For a few weeks it was Carlos Cortés at his chivalrous finest. When he asked Mom if he could move back in, she agreed. When he talked to Granddad about coming back into the business, he agreed, too. It appears that Granddad had grasped the future better than anyone else.

There were a few details to be dealt with. Like Dad's status in the company. Like changes in their home life. Like taping up fragile relationships after the vicious words that had been said and the secrets (or suppositions) that had been unearthed.

I don't know everything about these changes, but some were evident. Dad was named company vice president. Seven years later, in 1961, the Morris Hoffman Contracting Company became the Hoffman-Cortés Contracting Company. (This may also have had something to do with the fact that Gary was graduating from college and was about to join the company.) And there were other adjustments.

The one that struck me most when I came back for Christmas was that we now said grace at dinner, in a home where prayer of any sort had been conspicuously absent. Now we said it regularly, each night by a different family member.

During my visits, Gary and I contributed fairly mundane but personal prayers. Mom intoned hers with high drama, as if she were singing *La Bohème*. Dad always said the same traditional prayer, usually compressing it into three words: "Godisgood. Godisgreat. Letusthankyouforourfoodamen."

Then one night, when my grandparents were there, Dad mumbled his three words with unusual haste and disinterest. Grandma couldn't—or wouldn't—restrain herself. "That was certainly short and sweet," she said. Dad glowered. It was the last time I can remember my family saying grace.

Those are the facts. Now the stories. One of the agreements must have been that we would never, as a group, discuss the separation or reconciliation. For the next thirty years we tiptoed around it. If a family conversation accidentally began to veer in that direction, we assumed joint responsibility for steering it away.

But the protagonists privately told me their differing stories. I'll make them brief.

Dad: I stood up to the Hoffman clan and forced them to meet my terms if I were going to stay in the marriage and the company.

Mom: Dad got down on his hands and knees and begged me to take him back, which I did, but only under my conditions.

Grandma: I always wanted them to get back together, which is why I kept standing up for Carlos around Florence and encouraging Carlos to give it another chance.

Granddad: I'm glad Carlos came back.

All were probably both right and wrong. The reconciliation had occurred in a way that allowed all four of them to sleep with their illusions, if not snugly. Just as important, they could all tell their stories their ways while remaining within striking distance of the facts.

Gary and I were just happy to have our family back together, even if they weren't Ozzie and Harriet. But the summer of '54 had irremediably changed our family, twisting relationships into new forms that could not be straightened again. Myths had been destroyed. Revelations, once expressed, could no longer be ignored. Lived pain had given way to eternally painful memories.

That summer had brought a family earthquake. The next three decades would bring aftershocks. We all knew the fault lines were there, permanently.

The summer of '54 shook Mom in particular. In the fall of 1983, resting uncomfortably on the couch after chemotherapy treatment for lung cancer, out of nowhere Mom began privately telling my wife, Laurel, about the summer of '54. In those last days, she had to share the pain that had never left her and could never be discussed with members of the blood family.

As for me, the summer of '54 was a time of personal trans-
formation. It solidified my determination to never again live
in Kansas City. I went from being a naive, basically trusting
nineteen-year-old to becoming a suspicious, somewhat cynical
twenty-year-old. And I set foot on the road toward adulthood
bearing baggage I could never lay down.

37

Commencement

The first aftershock I witnessed came at my June 1956 graduation
from Cal. I hadn't spent much time in Kansas City since my folks'
reconciliation, so I was somewhat oblivious to the new family
landmines. Pauline helped detonate one of them.

We had broken off our engagement on December 31, 1954, an
appropriate ending to that tumultuous year. For the next eighteen
months we were on and off. By chance we had entered one of our
on-again phases when graduation rolled around.

The entire family, minus Granddad, came out to Berkeley. I
asked Pauline to join us for the ceremony and a post-graduation
family dinner, never giving a thought to clearing it with my folks.

Shortly after their arrival, I offhandedly mentioned that Pauline was joining us. Dad grinned. Mom grimaced. Gary didn't
care, one way or the other. Grandma flipped—her silence made it
clear that she was very upset.

On graduation day Grandma froze out Pauline, refusing to
say one word to her before, during, or after the ceremony in
Cal's Memorial Stadium. When it came time for dinner, Mom
informed me that Grandma had taken ill and couldn't go.

Actually, Grandma had just come down on Mom like a ton of
bricks for allowing me to ruin *her* graduation by including Pauline. Always the dutiful daughter, Mom told me—confidentially,

of course—how much I had hurt Grandma. Grandma wanted me to suffer, too.

Having been tutored by Dad on how to deal with such family gambits, I uttered the most perfunctory "Oh, that's too bad" when I learned about Grandma's dinner boycott. No more than that, because I knew Mom would run right back and tell Grandma if I showed any sign of real repentance.

After graduation, Grandma flew home, hardly speaking to me. But by the time the rest of us had driven back to Kansas City, sweet Grandma had returned. She never said another word to me about graduation. I never said anything about it to her. The sleeping dogs snored on.

As we parted, Pauline and I exchanged promises of enduring love and plans for my coming back out to see her. I never did.

* * *

Fourteen years later, in 1970, during one of my professional visits to Berkeley, I drove over to the two-story apartment house where Pauline had lived with her grandmother. The name, Perati—maybe hers, maybe her grandmother's—was still on the intercom. I stood there for several minutes, then decided not to ring.

38

Moving On

I never again lived in Kansas City. The summer of 1956, my last extended stay at home, served as a pit stop between my California undergraduate years and the rest of my life. I no longer saw the world through Kansas City family eyes or thought of it in strictly Kansas City family terms, which may help explain why I had stumbled into the graduation fiasco with Grandma and Pauline.

I remained close to my family and visited frequently. But as often as I returned home—yes, I still call it home—I sometimes felt sort of like an anthropologist who had gained the confidence of a distant yet strangely familiar tribe, enabling him to closely observe and surreptitiously learn about another culture's most intimate secrets.

Unaware of every Kansas City bump and throb, I began to view and interact with my family in new ways. Yet what I lost in intimacy from no longer being integral to the daily process, I gained by seeing the results more clearly. With each trip home I witnessed changes, sometimes significant ones, changes that might have been imperceptible had I been living permanently among the natives. Each time family members visited me in my new locations, I had new revelations.

Marriage, birth, death, and serendipity rearranged family relationships. Doors opened and closed—and sometimes slammed. Discoveries were made; hidden truths were laid bare; myths were shattered, and new myths took their place.

Graduation from Berkeley had brought the curtain down on the first act of my life. As I set out to make my way in the world—the world outside of Kansas City—I had no way of knowing how Kansas City, my family heritage, and my family's multicultural dance would continue to impel me in new and unexpected directions in my personal and professional life. Nor did I have any way of knowing that the ensuing years would create new, sometimes surprising connections to my family and my multiple heritages.

* * *

For more than a decade I wandered: New York City; Stratford, Connecticut; Fort Gordon, Georgia; Phoenix; Albuquerque; Pôrto Alegre and Rio de Janeiro, Brazil. In the process I picked up four more degrees in four different subjects, ending with an M.A. in Portuguese and Spanish and a Ph.D. in Latin American History from the University of New Mexico. I spent two years in the army writing press releases and held various other jobs, including public relations assistant for the American Shakespeare Festival and editor of the Phoenix Sunpapers weekly chain.

And, in 1961, I got married, to a Gentile named Murielle Jane Bunt, a tall, lovely, gracious English major at Arizona State University. We climbed mountains and read novels together.

Our wedding, held in a Phoenix community center, was conducted by a Maricopa County Superior Court judge. Murielle's devoutly Christian parents came. So did Mom, Dad, Grandma, Granddad, and Gary. Everybody behaved...or so I thought.

After reading a draft of this chapter, Gary told me a story I had never before heard. For our wedding, my family, including Bob and Sylvia Lewis from Berkeley, stayed at the same hotel. Over drinks and around the pool, when I was not there, Grandma, Granddad, and Mom repeatedly criticized me for marrying a Gentile. But Bob and Syl stuck up for me, saying that I was a good son and that they should support me in my decision.

Well, at least they behaved around Murielle and her family.

WORLDS FALL APART

39

The Wrong Kind of Jew

Despite their obvious disappointment that I had married a Gentile, from then on Mom, Grandma, and Granddad were very nice to Murielle. After all, they'd had plenty of years to prepare for this eventuality. Moreover, they still had my brother, Gary.

While a student at Rice Institute (later University), Gary became active in Hillel, the Jewish student organization. During his final year there he fell in love with Deborah Romotsky, a Jewish freshman from Long Island, New York, and they decided to get married. Especially after losing me to the goyim, Debby should have been the answer to a family prayer.

But she wasn't. Debby was a Conservative Jew—New York Conservative, meaning close to Kansas City Orthodox. For my Reform family, she was the wrong kind of Jew.

Mom and Grandma shared their worries with me. That Debby might lure Gary into Conservative Judaism. That she might publicly embarrass them by convincing Gary to join Beth Shalom,

Kansas City's Conservative synagogue. They responded to this religious threat with a ferocity that contrasted sharply with their resigned acceptance of my marriage to a Gentile. Tensions turned into confrontation in the fall of 1962 during Debby's first visit to Kansas City. I happened to be there.

Debby seemed very nice. Turns out she was. But she also seemed shy and fragile. Turns out she wasn't. She was just young (not quite eighteen) and overwhelmed by our family.

One night during a party at our house, Mom and Granddad took Gary and Debby back to Gary's bedroom and lit into them. They said Debby was too young and too Jewish. If she and Gary did get married, she was not to humiliate them by bringing her New York ways into our family. Gary and Debby must join *their* Reform temple, not the Conservative synagogue, or they would face the consequences. This hinted at exclusion from the construction company, which Gary had just joined. Debby came out from the room sobbing. Gary was ashen.

Less than ten months later, in June 1963, Gary and Debby got married on Long Island, with Saturday morning blessings at Debby's synagogue; a ritual-laden, very Conservative wedding ceremony; and a kosher wedding dinner. My whole family attended. I was Gary's best man. Even Dad wore a yarmulke.

In deference to the family—maybe partly out of fear of reprisal—Gary and Debby joined their Reform temple. But first appearances proved deceiving. Neither shy nor fragile, Debby turned out to be smart, determined, and patient, precisely the characteristics needed in long-range struggles with my family.

A year after they got married, Gary and Debby also joined Conservative Synagogue Beth Shalom. Mom, Grandma, and Granddad capitulated. Like Dad, they had grown weary of religious warfare. Even though they had lost both of their sons to the enemy, albeit different kinds of enemies, they adapted, more or less, to the new reality.

40

Temple Beth El

The religion story had yet another wrinkle. Grandma, Granddad, and Mom's vigorous reaction to Debby also reflected the fact that they, too, were going through their own religion-related traumas.

During the early 1950s their Reform congregation, Temple B'nai Jehudah, had decided to move from its old, midtown classical building to the growing south part of Kansas City. For the first stage of the move, a large school/administration building was completed in 1956. (The new sanctuary would not be built until 1967.)

As a long-standing Temple member, Granddad felt he should have been asked to do the construction. Instead he was told that he would have to submit a competitive bid. (Dad told me smugly that the building committee knew him too damn well to give him the job.)

Both hurt and angry, my family fumed, then quit the Temple. Two years later they became charter members of a new Reform congregation, Temple Beth El. The new temple now vied with the business as a major topic at family dinners.

At first, Grandma, Granddad, and Mom were in their glory. They rhapsodized about the warmth of the tiny (90 members) congregation compared to the huge (1,400 families), distant, formal B'nai Jehudah.

When Beth El built its own temple, it named the reception room the Morris and Ada Hoffman Hall. Mom gushed about how much Beth El's members respected Grandma and Granddad. Of course, the fact that they were the largest financial contributors may have also influenced that decision, although such thoughts remained unspoken.

But all institutions have conflicts. My family ended up becoming one of Beth El's major controversies.

While Grandma and Granddad were merely part of the monied crowd at B'nai Jehudah, they were the wealthiest family at Beth El. And they, especially Granddad, felt that being the major financial benefactors (as well as members of the governing board) gave them the right to make their wishes known—meaning known and obeyed.

The rabbi, in particular, grew tired of hearing their wishes, which could sound suspiciously like orders, and he became increasingly public with his frustrations. In response, Granddad announced at a family dinner that he was going to fire the rabbi, which he seemed to consider his prerogative.

The ranks of my family's enemies grew. A counterattack was inevitable. But how? And against whom? When the attack finally came, it involved another of my family's hot buttons—Mom's singing.

41

End of an Illusion

Singing brought Mom happiness. But like so many other things in her life, this joy was often bittersweet. Pleasure was muted by pain, some of it self-inflicted.

Growing up, Mom had taken singing lessons, and at Cal she had majored in music and foreign languages. Grandma and Granddad—especially Granddad, in whose eyes Mom could do no wrong—lavished praise on her voice. Before getting married, Mom and Dad had talked about a career in opera, although the unplanned arrival of yours truly had disrupted this dream.

I really don't know how good Mom's singing actually was. When I was young I thought she was pretty terrific, belting out songs at the piano, even songs that didn't call for belting. Over the years I learned that others—aside from our immediate family—rated her singing from okay to embarrassing.

Mom's main problem was that she thought she was something she wasn't. Or maybe she continued to think of herself as something she used to be.

Mom thought of herself as a lyric soprano. She may have started out that way, but her two-packs-a-day smoking, lunchtime martinis, and evening-long Scotch and sodas—and who knows what else—had shriveled her range and driven her voice down into the lower registers.

Mom's singing style didn't help, either. The word *pianissimo*, as in softly, didn't exist in her musical vocabulary. She sang like a Hoffman—bold, blunt, and unsubtle, even as she strained to reach high notes. In the four-person Temple B'nai Jehudah choir, you could always hear her booming voice, even when booming wasn't appropriate.

After Mom passed her second audition for membership in the Kansas City Music Club, shortly after World War II, she dove joyfully into club activities, like managing the advertising in the *Music Club Bulletin*. After being chosen for other offices in the Club, Mom set a goal of becoming president.

Then, one day, Mom came home unusually out of sorts. When I asked her what was wrong, she gave me a look that combined pain and bitterness. "Carlos, what I'm going to tell you isn't very pretty. I'm never going to become president of the Kansas City Music Club. One of my friends was going to nominate me, but was told, in no uncertain terms, that it wouldn't look right to have a Jew as president." She soon became inactive in the Club.

Mom also began getting small roles in local opera productions. Encouraged by her minor successes, she auditioned and was selected for a University of Kansas City summer opera workshop directed by Hans Schwieger, conductor of the Kansas City Philharmonic Orchestra. The workshop culminated in a performance of scenes from various operas.

At first Mom was excited by her roles, practicing them night after night at home. Then, one afternoon, she came home distraught. Schwieger had recast her as Maddalena in the quartet from *Rigoletto* and Mama Lucia in *Cavalleria Rusticana*. When I commented that these were fine roles, Mom became livid. "Those are for mezzo sopranos and contraltos. He took away all of my lyric soprano roles."

Then there was a long pause, accompanied by a look that told me more was on the way. "Do you know what else that son of a bitch Schwieger said? He told me my voice wasn't suited for a single lyric soprano role in all of grand opera! What do you think?" I quickly assured her that Schwieger didn't know what he was talking about, but my words provided little solace.

You see, Mom talked tough, but this bluster masked her deep-seated fragility. Schwieger's remarks had wounded her to the core and shattered her self-confidence. Mom finished the workshop and sang in the production, but never again auditioned for an opera.

The B'nai Jehudah choir became Mom's musical refuge. When she joined Temple Beth El, she became part of its choir and also sang more solos, despite the glaring evidence of her increasingly hoarse, nicotine-ravaged voice. Lacking the capacity for self-criticism when it came to her own singing, and constantly lauded by her folks, Mom was incapable of voluntarily remaining in the relative anonymity of the chorus.

Then came The Letter. It arrived at the house the day of a family dinner during one of my Kansas City visits.

Mom always opened her mail as soon as she came home from work. After she read this letter—and reread and reread it—she stopped, lit up a cigarette, and poured herself a Scotch. That should have been a tip-off. Mom habitually asked me to pour her a drink. This time she didn't, perhaps afraid her voice might crack. She took the letter back to her bedroom, remained there for a while, and then returned to cook dinner. But during the meal she abruptly took out the letter and read it to us.

The anonymous letter was short, direct, cowardly, vicious, and probably accurate. "Your voice is awful. You're ruining the services. You're the laughingstock of the Temple. You ought to quit singing."

Mom read the letter with wounded fury. She asked us what we thought of her voice, knowing we'd all tell her that she was great and to ignore the letter. Gary and I waxed eloquent about her singing. Dad supported her. Grandma consoled her. Granddad vowed revenge, despite not knowing whom to target.

Then Mom took over for herself. She had the best voice in the choir. She knew more about singing than all of the others put together. She'd be damned if anyone could scare her into quitting. Who in the hell were they to think they could frighten Florence Hoffman Cortés? We voiced our hearty support.

The conversation shifted to another topic, but Mom suddenly reopened the letter and read it aloud again. This was followed by her reiterated oath to not back down to their threats, and our reiterated encouragement to stick to her guns. Another shift in conversation, and then back to the letter. With each return, Mom's voice grew angrier and more anguished, while our support became more ritualized. Then I realized what was happening: that Mom would never sing publicly again.

Mom always appeared strong, poised, and ready to take on the world, and in many respects she was the family rock, the person upon whom we all relied. But she hadn't been blessed with Granddad's resilient courage and Grandma's will of steel. She could be hurt more easily, terrorized more effectively, and crushed more completely.

Despite the vehemence of her words, I knew she couldn't face standing up and singing again in front of the congregation, aware that one of the members had written the letter, that others probably knew about it, and that even more might share its sentiments. Maybe she also realized that the letter was basically correct, even if virulent and overstated. After all, the Temple chorus hardly qualified as grand opera.

But the letter wasn't just about Mom's voice, maybe not even *mainly* about her voice. It had as much—and maybe more—to do with a middle-class revolt against the Hoffman clan's wealth and sense of privilege. The easiest way to hurt the family was through Mom, its most vulnerable and sensitive member, and the simplest way to hurt Mom was by attacking her faltering voice. The coup worked.

Shortly thereafter, Mom, Grandma, and Granddad resigned from Beth El. A few years later, Grandma and Granddad quietly rejoined B'nai Jehudah, mainly so that they could attend High Holy Day services. Mom refused to follow them, saying it was a matter of principle.

From then on, the Jewish High Holy Days became a time of loneliness and torment for Mom. Each year she conducted her own solitary services at home. A few times I flew back to Kansas City to be with her.

42

Dad's Brain Surgery

The phone call from Kansas City came on a Friday afternoon in the early summer of 1965, while I was studying for my history doctoral orals at the University of New Mexico. Dad's doctor had discovered a massive brain tumor. Surgery was scheduled for Monday, with an only 15 percent chance of Dad's surviving the surgery, and a less than 5 percent chance of his having much of a brain left, even if he did survive. Early Saturday morning, Murielle and I flew to Kansas City.

Given Mom's increased lack of resiliency, I expected the worst. Instead I found her surprisingly calm, as if drawing on reserves of character that had lain dormant during the Beth El furor.

Dad seemed almost relaxed, at times even jocular. Once again, as he had done more than two decades earlier following his leg injury, he received the last rites. Once again, he prepared to confront death with steely determination.

We spent most of the weekend in Dad's hospital room. When we left on Sunday evening, we said we'd be back early the next morning to be with him before he went into surgery at eleven a.m. Yet as unprepared as I was for Mom's calmness in the face of Dad's likely death, I was equally as unprepared for the next morning's bizarre proceedings.

Mom had learned well from Grandma, a creature of habit who was most comfortable when following a set routine. But Mom had magnified that penchant into a mania for relentlessly adhering to rigid ways of doing almost everything, including breakfast.

Murielle and I got up early Monday morning, ready to rush over to the hospital for those few precious hours with Dad, possibly our last ones. Mom, however, had already launched into her elaborate breakfast-preparing routine. So we ate. And then she went into her equally elaborate kitchen-cleaning routine, even as we pleaded with her that time was racing by and we wanted to see Dad.

But nothing—not Dad, not the unforgiving ticking of the second hand, not our pleading to leave the dishes or at least to let us help her—could dislodge Mom from her predetermined path. She simply could not leave until she had done what she had become accustomed to doing every morning, even though this was not every morning. Not until ten-fifteen did we get to the hospital. By the time we parked and walked to Dad's room, we had less than thirty minutes with him before they wheeled him out, maybe to die.

But he didn't. Miraculously, that human bulldog whipped death again.

Murielle and I stayed on for another week until Dad had traversed the critical stages of recovery from surgery. By the time we returned to Albuquerque, we knew Dad was going to live, but not how much of Dad would survive.

Frequent phone calls from Mom assured me that Dad was making progress. He was beginning to talk. He could recall some things. But the tone of Mom's voice didn't convey much assurance.

A few days before my doctoral orals, the phone rang. It was the voice of a stranger. He spoke haltingly, responding as if he had heard only bits of what I was saying. But it was Dad.

As soon as I passed my oral exams, Murielle and I headed for Kansas City, dragging a U-Haul van. I had received a Ford Foundation Foreign Area Fellowship to spend a semester at Columbia University and then twenty months conducting dissertation research in Brazil. Since we had been living in a furnished apartment, we didn't have much stuff besides clothes, books, notes, and—I should add—six Siamese cats, including four babies. Mom said we could store our excess in the garage. Unfortunately, that didn't include the cats, whom we ultimately distributed to friends and Murielle's parents.

My trepidation grew as we neared Kansas City. Dad answered the door. Thinner, paler, unsteady, slow-talking. But there. Dad had made it.

And Mom? Mom the rock had returned, at least temporarily— but not as just a rock. She was gentler, more considerate, more supportive. Feeling more needed, Mom had answered the call.

Questions remained. How far would Dad come back? Would he be able to return to the business? How would all of this affect his relationship with Granddad? But at least Dad was still with us to make those questions worth asking.

43

Recovery

Dad clawed his way back, slowly. Conversations remained a struggle, with long silences as Dad searched in frustration for obvious words. Listeners faced a delicate balance between waiting too long, thereby adding to his frustration, or moving on too quickly, thereby exposing his defeat.

Mom was doing well under stress, but she couldn't avoid Hoffman overkill. Rightfully proud of Dad's determined comeback, she talked about it repeatedly, sometimes in private but too often in front of Dad, and with irritating exaggeration. Dad's eyes screamed, "Damn it, Florence. Enough already!" That proud man well knew what he wasn't, and he wasn't nearly what he had been.

Dad was a Civil War buff. One night a TV quiz show featured the Civil War as its special topic. Mom made us all sit down to watch it, proclaiming that Dad probably knew more than any of the contestants. But as question after question passed, with Dad unable to answer, his frustration grew. During a commercial, he announced that he had to go to the bathroom. We didn't see him again until the next morning.

Still, Dad made progress. He began driving, going to the office, even traveling a bit. When Murielle and I left for Brazil in early 1966, my folks promised to come down for a visit. They did, in early 1967.

Together we visited Uruguay, Argentina, Chile, and Peru, even flying into the Andes to see Cuzco and Machu Picchu. Travel allowed Mom and Dad to be a more loving, devoted couple. Watching them cavort on the road, almost like little kids, made it clear how much Kansas City weighed on them. Free from concerns about family and image, they simply had fun, and despite the language barrier, they charmed our Brazilian friends.

Occasionally, Mom's manias intruded. She withdrew into one of her silent pouts in a nice Montevideo restaurant, refusing to eat her fine steak dinner because it smelled as if someone had cut it with a fish knife (it didn't smell that way to the rest of us). And despite warnings about the extreme effects of alcohol at high altitudes, she had to spend a day in bed in Cuzco after overindulging in pisco sours.

Dad's traveling downside was even sadder. It was his Spanish— or more accurately, his lack of it, an aftereffect of brain surgery.

For the sake of Dad's pride, I tried to let him take the lead when ordering meals, dealing with cabbies, asking for directions, and getting through customs. But after a few mishaps—receiving the wrong food or ending up at an undesired location—I had to be ready to take charge. We didn't dare send him out on solo missions.

Considering his pre-surgery prognosis, Dad had made a remarkable comeback. But during that trip I realized that I would probably never again know the demanding intellectual and ethical mentor who had guided, challenged, and encouraged me throughout my Kansas City years.

* * *

Dad had recovered enough to return to the office. But not enough to deal with the next challenge that would come his way.

When Mom and Dad had reunited after their 1954 split, Granddad had accepted Dad back into the business. There was no joy or celebration. It was simply an adjustment to the fact that Dad was still married to his daughter and was the father of his grandsons.

But Granddad had vowed that Dad would never become head of the company. Despite occasional talk about Granddad becoming chairman of the board, he refused to give up his presidency.

Then along came my brother, Gary. With his engineering education and his outgoing, hail-fellow-well-met personality, he became a great addition to the company. Granddad loved introducing him to associates and clients as "My grandson, the engineer."

Above all, Gary was blood family, which counted for just about everything in Granddad's eyes. So when Dad's surgery provided the opening, Granddad named himself chairman of the board and vaulted Gary over Dad into the company presidency, with Dad remaining vice president.

Dad was hurt, but he lacked the will to put up any real fight. Moreover, he was very proud of Gary. And at least a Cortés now held the company presidency.

NEW BEGINNINGS

44

Riverside

In January 1968, a month after Murielle and I returned from Brazil, I began teaching at the University of California, Riverside. In September of that year our daughter, Alana, was born.

I had no great ambitions or career master plan. Just to teach, write, do research—normal history professor stuff. Maybe move on to another university if an interesting offer came along.

There was no way to foresee that I would stay at UCR until early retirement in 1994 and would remain in Riverside for more than forty years. Even less predictable was that events—in Riverside and in Kansas City—would radically alter my professional life, my relationship to my family, and my personal connection to my ethnic and religious heritages.

Shortly after I began teaching, I received a phone call from a fellow professor named Eugene Cota-Robles, an eminent microbiologist. His voice betrayed a certain hesitancy, but he finally got around to asking the big question. He had noticed my name among the new UCR faculty and wondered if I happened to be Mexican American.

I answered in the affirmative, with caveats. Gene asked me to meet him for lunch, at which time I explained the caveats. The Jewish side of my family. My limited contact with Kansas City's Mexican American community while I was growing up. My less-than-perfect Spanish. But Gene seemed unfazed. I qualified.

UCR, circa 1968, was hardly a minority hotbed. There were fewer than 150 Mexican American students on a campus of 4,500. There were only two Black faculty members, and Gene had been the only Chicano. My arrival doubled the Chicano faculty ranks.

Over lunch, Gene explained his situation. He was directing the Educational Opportunity Program, an outreach program for minority and poor students. Would I be willing to become involved? And he was forming a new student organization, the United Mexican-American Students (UMAS). Would I be willing to help?

These requests came at a less-than-opportune time. I was under tremendous pressure to complete my dissertation by June 1969 or my appointment would be terminated. The wise answer would have been "no." The irrepressible answer was "yes." I never looked back.

When I accompanied Gene to my first UMAS meeting, my fair-skinned, hazel-eyed looks caused predictable and understandable consternation among the students. I became a sort of provisional member of the clan, sensing an implicit requirement: *it's up to you to prove that you're really one of us.* And who knows? Maybe my newly grown beard and snot-colored moustache—a mercifully brief and certifiably ridiculous cosmetic experiment—gave me a bit of credibility.

But full acceptance was something else. Wait a minute. Hadn't I left that concern behind? Sixteen years after high school, why was I again searching for acceptance, this time from a bunch of undergraduates—barely half my age—who might not consider

me brown enough? Whatever. I wanted acceptance, and ultimately got it.

In the winter of 1970, I taught the first Chicano History course
ever offered at UCR. Two years later, during the spring of 1972,
I received an enticing offer from the nearby Claremont Colleges.
But a group of Chicano students came to my home, asked me to
stay at UCR, and appealed to me to become chair of UCR's Mexican-American Studies Program (soon to become Chicano Studies).
I stayed and served as chair for the next seven and a half years.

Dad had worked hard to deepen my attachment to my Mexican roots. Maybe my decision to embrace the Chicano part of my
heritage was his ultimate family victory. And, in a stroke of fate,
it would also create an additional bond between us.

* * *

But even as my UCR experiences were deepening my Chicano
attachments, other circumstances serendipitously added another
dimension to my professional life. In the fall of 1971, the California textbook wars erupted. The state was in the process of adopt-
ing history and social studies textbooks for grades five through
eight. Section 9305 of the State Education Code mandated that,
to be adopted, textbooks must "correctly portray the role and contributions of the Negro and other ethnic groups," a turn of phrase
worthy of being encased in a time capsule.

The Los Angeles Unified School District's Black and Mexican
American Education Commissions reviewed the textbooks and
testified that they failed to meet the Education Code standard.
In response, the California State Board of Education created a
thirteen-member task force, mainly university faculty, to review
the textbooks. I was one of those chosen.

For more than a month we held weekly Friday and Saturday meetings. It was like a post-graduate seminar, in which task
force members voiced their concerns and provided insights about
the textbook treatment of various ethnic groups. Our report

recommended extensive changes; a few were implemented before the inevitable adoption.

Serving on the task force not only prodded me intellectually, but also brought back memories of the ethnic and religious convulsions of my Kansas City youth—our family conflicts, a thwarted Bar Mitzvah, fraternity rejections, being renamed "Carl," and class divisions at Philmont.

Then came the aftermath. The textbook controversy received considerable publicity. I began receiving invitations to speak about the adoption process and the issue of ethnic content of textbooks. Two years after launching my Chicano History course, I was being drawn rapidly and inexorably into the inchoate field of multicultural education. I enthusiastically embraced this new venture.

In four years my professional directions had changed dramatically. My friendship with Gene and my work with Chicano students had deepened my Mexican attachment and injected something new into my life—a commitment to a larger social purpose. The textbook task force had expanded my vista into diversity writ large. I had found my professional calling: to draw upon my role as a scholar to try to make things better for people—individuals and groups—who had been marginalized. And with my new professional calling came a further understanding of myself and my family.

* * *

T. S. Eliot wrote, "We had the experience but missed the meaning." Having taken a long Kansas City multicultural journey, I was finally beginning to understand its broader meaning.

Things that would have caused me pain in the past now began to bring me pleasure. I started enjoying the fact that I was a *huero* (a light-skinned Latino). So what if it made me a bit marginal— among both Latinos and Anglos? Being doubly marginal as a teenager at Southwest High was horrendous. Being multiply marginal as an adult in California was becoming a delight.

Once, I was invited by an Anglo who had never met me to give a luncheon talk at a statewide education conference. On the day of the conference, when he saw my name tag, his face dropped. Caught off guard, he couldn't restrain himself from saying what others may have thought and suppressed: "Uh, we were hoping for someone, uh, a little darker." I was ready with an answer (adapted from Neil Simon's *The Goodbye Girl*). "This year I'm working on younger. Next year I'll work on darker."

45

Mr. Chicano

I'm not sure when it was that Dad became a Chicano, too. Or when he became a Republican. They both happened around the same time.

When my folks picked me up at the airport during my first Kansas City visit after starting at UCR, a Nixon-Agnew sticker blared from their bumper.

Nixon? A guy Dad had always referred to as "Tricky Dick"? Dad, who had been a passionate Roosevelt Democrat, had voted for Truman against Dewey in 1948, and had supported Kennedy against Nixon in 1960?

When I expressed consternation, Mom answered, almost matter-of-factly: "After all, your Dad is a leader of the Kansas Republican Party." A Nixon-Agnew bumper sticker? Dad a leader of the Kansas Republican Party? Had I landed in *The Twilight Zone*?

It turns out Mom was right, sort of. If titles mean status, Dad was a leader. He had been named associate vice chairman of the Republican State Committee, a post he retained for the better part of a decade. But why? And how?

According to Mom, Dad had been selected because he was a prominent leader of the Kansas Hispanic community. A what?

Sure, Dad was proudly Mexican, but he'd had relatively little local involvement.

The fates, however, had converged on him. Following the success of the Democratic Party's 1960 "Viva Kennedy" campaign, Republicans were making a tepid effort to reach out to Latinos. By the late 1960s, this meant featuring a few Spanish surnames in party leadership lists. Dad fit the profile.

He was known in the Kansas City business world, had earned civic eminence through his Boy Scout service, and did have friends among local Latino entrepreneurs. Need I add that he also had enough money to make expected party donations and attend expensive political functions. Ergo, Dad was just the kind of financially solid, socially acceptable Latino with whom the real Kansas Republican leadership could be comfortable. As Debby put it, "He was in the right place at the right time with the right surname." I would add, "with the right bank account."

This political opportunity had arrived just as Granddad was marginalizing Dad in the company. So when the Republican Party beckoned, he answered the call. And he didn't even have to ride a horse.

Dad now referred to himself as a Chicano. Like me, Dad had found personal fulfillment by identifying with other Mexican Americans. He was sincerely trying to help "his people"…in his conservative way.

One time I took him to a Riverside Chicano gathering where a militant speaker began ranting against "Mexicans who sell out to Anglos." Looking at me with a blend of disgust and boredom, Dad switched off his hearing aid.

During every conversation, by phone or in person, Dad brought me up to date on his Chicano wheelings and dealings. How he had become vice president of Kansas City's Hispanic Chamber of Commerce and a member of the Kansas Human Rights Commission. How he had helped heal a community split between two Chicano organizations, United American Mexicans (United AM) and United Mexican Americans (UNIMEX). And every time I went to Kansas City, Dad would show me off to his Latino Republican buddies and brag about his son, the Chicano Studies chair.

Dad's office changed. Down came business commendations and pictures of construction projects. Up went photos of Dad with Dick Nixon, Spiro Agnew, George Bush, Bob Dole, and just about any other Republican dignitary who wanted a picture shaking hands with a Mexican.

Dad and Mom even attended the 1972 and 1976 Republican National Conventions, with Dad a Kansas alternate delegate. He even received a paragraph in *Time* magazine's coverage of the 1972 convention. Described as "silver-haired Carlos Cortes" (no accent), he was quoted as saying: "I want to see others achieve what I have. The opportunity is here. The system is good. I'm sold on it."

Just as Dad was in his element, so was Mom in hers. A professional at burning bridges, Mom had become alienated from one activity after another—the Kansas City Music Club, local opera productions, Temple B'nai Jehudah, and later Temple Beth El. Dad's emergence on the political stage had rescued Mom from social oblivion. It was full speed ahead. Republican events abounded. Now she could drop names with ease—state legislators, congressmen, cabinet members, even the president.

As tokenistic as their whole political interlude may have been, this Republican flirtation was great for Mom and Dad. Through politics they shared a decade in the imagined limelight.

The immaculate ethnic compromise hammered out during my teenage years —the compromise that had not prevented the summer of '54—finally seemed to have borne fruit. Dad had me, his fellow Chicano son. Mom, Grandma, and Granddad had Gary to carry on their Judaism, albeit a more Conservative Judaism than they wished. Everyone had made some sort of peace with our makeshift family arrangements, even taking pride in each others' accomplishments, although their choices might at times grate on personal beliefs. Our family was nearing its high water mark.

46

Family Man

My relocation to Riverside gave Dad a way to reconnect to his native California. It also spurred him into a greater effort to reach out to his brothers and sisters.

For three decades he had seldom seen them. They never came to Kansas City. Except during my four years at Cal, he only occasionally went out to California to visit them. Letters and phone calls were sporadic. Now that I was living in California, Dad tried to recapture something that had eluded him during his isolation in Kansas City—a deeper, truer sense of Cortés family.

Four of Dad's siblings were still in California—Eduardo and Alejandro in Northern California, Susana in San Diego, and Vicente in nearby Garden Grove. (His other sister, Elena, was still living in Puerto Vallarta.) The trips to Northern California and to San Diego worked out well. Then there was Vinnie.

It should have been the epitome of brothers reuniting, since Vinnie lived only an hour from Riverside. But it didn't work out that way because of what turned out to be a Cortés family habit—a cavalier attitude toward time coupled with a nonchalance about inconveniencing others.

Before getting to know Dad's brothers, I had assumed this was just one of Dad's idiosyncrasies—making arrangements without consulting with or even informing Mom, often leaving her holding the bag. Like telling her at the last minute that he had invited people over for dinner or drinks.

Dad's siblings dealt with time in a similarly cavalier manner, but Dad upped the ante because he was the oldest son, a big deal in the traditional Mexican family. Meaning that he deserved the special respect due the oldest brother.

When Dad came out for a visit, he would call his two Southern California siblings *after* he had arrived. This worked fine for

Susie, who, with advanced diabetes, was mostly at home. But it didn't go down well with Vinnie, who was running his own business and became increasingly unappreciative of Dad's "I'm here" calls asking him (make that, ordering him) to get together during his few days in town.

The first few times Dad did this, Vinnie adjusted his schedule. We would either drive down fifty miles to Garden Grove or Vinnie and his family would drive up to Riverside for a day. But every visit ended with Vinnie asking Dad to let him know in advance next time so they could avoid scheduling conflicts. Each time the request became more emphatic.

My folks spent Christmas 1974 with Murielle, Alana, and me. As usual, Dad called Vinnie when he got to Riverside, told him he was going to be in town for a few days, and said Vinnie should come up and see him. I could tell from Dad's end of the conversation that Vinnie didn't say yes, but didn't say no either. Probably something on the order of "I've already got plans for the next few days, but I'll call you if I can change my schedule." Dad translated Vinnie's response as Yes. I translated it as No. I was right.

Vinnie never came. Or called. Every day Dad would mumble, with declining conviction, "I've got a feeling Vinnie will be coming up today." Every day added to my conviction, not only that Vinnie wouldn't come, but that he was so pissed at Dad that he wouldn't even call him back. It was Vinnie's unspoken declaration of independence from Dad. Cortés stubbornness on both sides.

Dad returned to Kansas City more hurt than disappointed. Not seeing Vinnie was hardly a tragedy. Not having Vinnie pay him his proper younger-brotherly obeisance was a dagger in the heart. And for Vinnie not even to show him the courtesy of a phone call was unpardonable.

So Dad refused to pardon Vinnie for not calling to say he wasn't coming up to see him. And Vinnie refused to pardon Dad for not calling earlier from Kansas City. They stopped calling—or writing—for ten years.

47

Granddad Dies

Dad had found new meaning in life—his reinvigorated Mexican-ness, his new Chicano identity, his dalliance with Republican politics, his reconnection with California, his somewhat-conflicted reestablishment of family ties, and his stronger ethnic bond with me.

Granddad, too, had found greater peace. Now in his eighties, comfortable with Gary running the company when he was gone, and with Dad firmly consigned to his place, Granddad began to take more time off. He and Grandma started spending part of each winter in Palm Springs, an hour's drive from Riverside, so my family spent long weekends with them. There were good times, but they didn't last long. In the fall of 1972, I received another Kansas City phone call. Granddad had contracted colon cancer.

I visited Kansas City three times before the end. Each time I found less and less of that formidable man who had taught me to play gin rummy and introduced me to cigars. The man who could be gruff and rigid, but also generous and loving. The man who would take me on inspections of his jobs, hoping to interest me so that I would follow in his footsteps. The man who hoped I would marry a Jewish girl, but was ultimately supportive when I didn't.

In one of those ironies that should make us pause to think about the site of ultimate control, Granddad's hospital room happened to look down on one of his company's jobs. By turning on his side, he could watch carpenters, plumbers, plasterers, laborers, and hod carriers with whom he had worked, whom he had berated, and whom he had complimented minutes later with deepest sincerity. He could even call the job superintendent, which he did several times a day…at first.

But by Christmastime Granddad didn't bother to call any more. He didn't have the energy, or maybe he just lacked the will.

In early January, Granddad abruptly asked Gary to pull down the window shade. He never again looked at the job site.

Granddad died in February 1973. When I went back for his funeral, I was prepared for family grief. But I wasn't prepared for the fact that grief now shared the stage with fear, bordering on terror, about Granddad's funeral.

With their hypertrophied vision of Granddad's importance, Mom and Grandma had chosen the Temple B'nai Jehudah sanctuary for the ceremony—a towering, cavernous room with seating for seven hundred. (In the future we wisely chose a far more intimate funeral home chapel.) Then reality set in.

Who might actually come? People from the Girl Scouts, for whom he had done extensive volunteer work in developing their summer camp? Maybe. Their Saturday night poker club? Many of them had already died. The men who worked for Granddad? Sure, if they were given the day off. But how about his other friends and business associates? This translated into unaskable questions. Did he really have that many friends? Would his business associates actually show up?

Mom had always described Granddad as a tough, aggressive businessman who could drive hard bargains but always earned respect and affection. Dad had a slightly different image of him. Granddad was a mean son of a bitch who alienated just about everyone with whom he did business. Granddad probably fell somewhere in between Mom's adulation and Dad's cynicism.

As the clock wound down to the funeral, Mom became terrified that maybe Dad was right and that, like Willy Loman in *Death of a Salesman*, Granddad would go to his grave with few witnesses. The night before the funeral Mom could talk about nothing else. How would everyone know that Granddad had died (how does anyone know)? The five-and-a-half-inch-long newspaper obituary was too short (isn't it always?). The Kansas City paper had buried it in an obscure place (the third notice in the obituary section). What could we do about the weather (it usually happens)?

117

Mom worked the phones like a desperate campaign manager on election eve, inviting, pleading, begging, cajoling, and browbeating anyone she could reach. With each victory she would inform us that so-and-so would be at the funeral. With each defeat she would come in, Scotch and cigarette in hand, to tell us about another ungrateful bastard who couldn't—or wouldn't—be there.

I went to bed praying, for Mom's and especially Grandma's sakes, that hordes of Morris Hoffman–lovers would descend on B'nai Jehudah, filling the huge sanctuary to standing-room-only capacity. I also knew there wasn't a chance in hell this would happen.

The day was bitterly cold with layers of ice and snow. When our funeral limousine arrived at B'nai Jehudah, few tire tracks and only a smattering of cars greeted us in the parking lot. "It's still twenty minutes until the funeral and most people don't show up early," I comforted Mom in my most convincing voice, which couldn't have convinced anyone. Grandma was in a trance.

The family grieving room sat off to the side of the pulpit, without a view of the sanctuary, mercifully. As the service ended, Mom was like a caged animal, eager to leap onto the pulpit to see who—make that how many—had come to pay their respects. But by the time the rabbi had visited the grieving room and given us his last condolences, the sanctuary had emptied. A few people were talking in the back.

I interjected that there must have been hundreds at the service. When hundreds of names didn't appear in the funeral register, I assured Mom that lots of people show up just in time for the funeral, go straight in, and never sign the book.

Yet there were only a few dozen people at Rose Hill, the Temple's cemetery—mainly some of Granddad's longtime employees. There were few business associates or even poker club members. Again I assured Mom, this time pontificating that most people who go to funerals don't also go to the cemetery, particularly in the middle of a business day. Mom accepted that explanation more readily because of the many times she and Granddad had done just that.

How many people actually came to the funeral? I don't know. But I was thankful that my family couldn't see the sanctuary. Illusions, or at least rationalizations, are often much better than reality.

A few days after the funeral I went out to the cemetery to visit Granddad, alone. It was late in the afternoon. I don't know why, but I sort of expected to see his casket still sitting there, even though we had seen them lower his body and I had even shoveled some dirt on the casket as part of the burial ritual. For some reason I wasn't prepared to find merely a flat piece of ground.

I remember talking to Granddad, but I haven't the faintest idea what I said. That moment made the word *finality* really mean something. Granddad was gone, for good.

From that moment on, Rose Hill would play a plangent role in my life. Other family members had already been buried in what had become a Hoffman-Weinsaft extended family plot. But this was different.

Then I realized how cold it was. And how cold I felt.

SURVIVING GRANDDAD

48

Readjustment

Granddad's death taught me a simple lesson—with every family death, a new family is born.

We all had to adjust. To the loud empty space at the family dinner table. To the crowded solitude of Grandma's apartment. To her fear of traveling alone.

The family team reorganized, smoothly, nearly silently. Gary took charge of the business. Dad became his second banana, even being promoted to chairman of the board. Mom served as Grandma's rock. Debby provided support, while I became a distant role player. The family didn't need a coach.

We were all concerned about Grandma. But she bounced back like the champ we knew—a tiny, eighty-one-year-old porcelain figure lined with steel.

Grandma remained in her spacious, memory-haunted twenty-first-floor apartment in the Sulgrave, a Country Club Plaza high-rise overlooking Loose Park, where I had gone to make out on dates when I was in high school. Granddad had left her well fixed financially, although she took pleasure in complaining about the cost of things. She went out less often, mainly for family functions, but the phone rang constantly and visitors came frequently.

She continued in the poker club. But because so many other men in the club preceded and followed Granddad to the grave, the gender imbalance turned Saturday nights into what they called "hen parties." Too few roosters. Male recruitment became a top club priority. Grandma even joked to me that the first thing club women did in the morning was read the obituaries to see if some Jewish wife had died, thereby increasing the pool of eligible men for the poker table.

Grandma's new, darker sense of humor announced that she'd make it. She did, for twelve more years. And I—her goyim-marrying grandson—helped fulfill her long-deferred, deepest Jewish dream.

49

Israel

I'm not sure when I decided to take Grandma to Israel. For years she'd asked Granddad, who invariably said yes, next year. But next year was always too busy, so he never got around to it.

Age and arthritis were rapidly closing Grandma's window of opportunity. So in typical Cortés style—without discussing it with anyone—I went to her apartment and asked her if she'd like to go.

That night over dinner I offhandedly mentioned that, by the way, I was taking Grandma to Israel. Dad looked nonplussed, as if he had just lost his Chicano son. Mom became infuriated, screaming her traditional "Why didn't you talk to me first? You're just like your father." She seemed sort of embarrassed that she hadn't come up with the idea herself.

As soon as Mom calmed down, she announced that she would join us on the trip. Fine with me. She also asked Dad if he wanted to go, eliciting a string of expletives.

So in March of 1975, the three of us headed for Israel. On our first morning in Tel Aviv, we were picked up by Rafi Golran, our attentive, knowledgeable personal guide, who led us through Israel with an ingratiating blend of information and irony, fact and legend, civic pride and cynicism.

Other than just getting Grandma to the promised land, I had a specific goal in mind. Since shortly after World War II, Grandma had helped fund an orphanage for children of Holocaust victims. The orphanage was just south of Tel Aviv, so I asked Rafi to take us there first.

In front of the orphanage stood a wall with large plaques bearing the names of the major contributors. I took pictures of Grandma standing in front of the wall, the letters ADA HOFF-MAN fully visible behind her. The look on Grandma's face made the entire trip worthwhile. Everything else was a bonus. Then it was off for three weeks of tourism, with some surprising ethnic interludes.

First came a Jerusalem Passover Seder with the family of a young Israeli who had attended college in Kansas. It was a Sephardic Seder, of descendants of Jews who had been expelled from Spain in the fifteenth century. My family was Ashkenazic, following Eastern European religious traditions.

Ashkenazic Seders are fun but formal and highly ritualized. Our Sephardic Seder was more like a jam session—casual, free flowing, improvisational. I found it a blast; Mom and Grandma considered it blasphemous. They disapproved, as they did with most things that weren't done exactly their way.

Then, a couple of days later, while exploring Jerusalem alone, I discovered the Buenos Aires Restaurant, a large house set back from the street. Grandma didn't show any interest, so Mom and

I went there for lunch...except the door was locked, defying
the posted business hours. Undaunted, I knocked several times.
Finally the owner answered and told me, in English, that the restaurant was closed temporarily for remodeling.

Detecting a recognizable accent, I responded in Portuguese. The
man's eyes lit up. In a few seconds we exchanged the vital information, that he was from Brazil and that I had lived there. He insisted
we come in. When he came back from the kitchen with his Mexican chef, we learned that the chef had worked at Hotel San José
Purua, the spa at which I had met Tía Anita and Tío Salvador.

With our Latino connections established, they wouldn't let us
leave. The owner opened a bottle of wine and the cook insisted on
making samples of his Mexican food. Before long we were sharing
stories in Spanish, Portuguese, and English, including the chef's
tribulations in trying to prepare Latin American food—mainly
Mexican—using uncooperative Israeli ingredients, for unappreciative Israeli palates.

Walking back to the hotel, Mom and I talked as real pals in
a way we had seldom done since I had gone off to college. And
I caught a glimpse of the enchanting might-have-been Florence Hoffman, maybe a facsimile of the young woman with
whom Dad had fallen in love. Maybe the woman she would have
become had life taken a different course.

* * *

I suppose my story might be better if the trip had caused me to
rediscover my Jewish roots (I'd never lost them) and brought
me back to Judaism (it didn't). Sorry, no soaring music. But it
did deepen a sense of personal connection to my ancestral histories, much as my trips to Mexico had done. I was becoming
more comfortable with, even relishing, my ethnic and religious
multiplicity.

The Israel visit also added a new strand of reconnection to my
family. For three weeks I reveled in being with a mother and

grandmother not weighed down by the burden of being in Kansas City, with its unrelenting imposition of expectations, obligations, limitations, and calcified relationships. I was with two wonderful, loving, temporarily liberated women basking in the freedom of being themselves, if only too briefly.

Our Israel experiences became our private treasure, which nobody else could ever experience, at least the way we did. Mom and I seeing Grandma in front of her orphanage wall. Me watching Mom clambering around Masada and floating in the Dead Sea. The three of us strolling around a kibbutz together. Only occasionally did Grandma inject a wistful "Your grandfather would have loved this trip."

* * *

Our plane ticket permitted us to spend a few days in either Athens or Rome on our way home. Mom and Grandma chose Rome. Caesar over Plato. Nero over Aristotle. Caligula over Socrates. Lions 3, Hemlock 0.

By chance we were traveling home on Easter weekend. How could we pass up a chance to spend Easter Sunday with the Pope (and a few others) in Vatican Square? The opportunity to participate in this spectacular touched Mom's operatic soul.

Dad had gotten the Kansas City diocese bishop to write us a letter of introduction. Mom assured me this would guarantee special treatment at Easter Sunday Mass. This didn't quite square with my TV visions of crowds jamming Vatican Square, but so what?

With tired Grandma resting in our Rome hotel, Mom and I took a cab to the address on the bishop's letter, a small office a few blocks from the enormous Victor Emmanuel Monument and the Colosseum. One of the functionaries cursorily looked at the letter and then grabbed two printed cards from a huge box. The cards invited us (no name) to the Easter Sunday Papal Mass. Before we left the office, more than a dozen other people had entered and picked up their "special" invitations.

Mom seemed a bit taken aback by the profligate distribution of invitations, so I suggested we get to Mass early on Sunday. Mom translated this to mean Kansas City early.

I had forgotten about Mom's morning rituals. Putting on her face. A leisurely breakfast. Endless cajoling of Grandma about how we would be just fine, when we would get back, and what she should do in case we disappeared into the entrails of Rome. (I considered adding "in case I decide to convert to Catholicism," but I restrained myself.)

When we finally reached Vatican Square, we found about half of the Catholic world already there. Early for them didn't mean the same as for Mom. "I wonder where our special section is?" asked Mom, squeezing her two treasured invitations. I didn't have the heart to mention the bottomless box of cards we had seen two days earlier. We wormed our way into the crowd on the fringes of the square, but I could tell from Mom's face that her staying power was eroding with every bump, elbow, jostle, and whiff of bad breath.

Well, nothing ventured, nothing gained. Or is it fools rush in? Never mind. It was time for the two-minute drill.

I began shouting in Portuguese, Spanish, English, and every other language I had ever brushed up against. Tugging Mom and waving the invitations as wildly as I could, I inched forward.

Then, magically, the bodies parted. Moses, Charlton Heston, and Cecil B. DeMille together couldn't have done a better job on the Red Sea. A narrow corridor appeared, created by papal guards in their extravagant Renaissance uniforms, complete with helmets and lances. At the front of the corridor some functionary was wildly waving his arms, beckoning whomever to come forward, seemingly unconcerned about who had invitations. Forward we went, along with a bunch of others who joined in the mad dash for pay dirt.

We passed through the human corridor, up a ramp, and suddenly found ourselves standing on an elevated stage directly in front of the Vatican, beside a few dozen long wooden benches.

Soon we were sitting on one of them. No logical explanation. The triumph of will, audacity, and dumb luck.

The benches sat perpendicular to the Vatican, which rose majestically to our right. To our left were the masses packing Vatican Square. Some twenty yards in front us of stood an elevated altar and, soon, the Pope.

Mom was in her element. Grinning from ear to ear, she periodically squeezed my elbow, an irritating habit she displayed whenever she wanted to let you know she was feeling emotion. But I didn't ask her to stop, as I sometimes did, since she was savoring the moment. I half expected her to break into a chorus of "If My Friends Could See Me Now." Fortunately she didn't.

So there we were. My good Jewish mother, smacked in the face by her two Kansas City temples, alienated by the Sephardic Seder, now a few yards from the Pope and exulting in the Vatican ambience. And me, her religiously wayward son, here while my Mexican father lodged his silent protest by remaining in Kansas City.

It was the culmination of our trip and maybe a trope for our four-decade family journey. For me the Israel–Rome trip had been a multicultural grand slam.

50

Laurel

My personal life had its bumps, too. My marriage to Murielle blessed me with a wonderful daughter, Alana Madrugada, born in 1968, and it ended in divorce in 1978.

That same year I remarried—to Laurel Vermilyea Riley, a warm, witty, intelligent, serenely beautiful, calmly vivacious young lady from Carlsbad, California. Every day she brings me joy. Dad and Mom fell in love with her, too. So, ultimately, did Grandma.

With her relaxed, outgoing nature and her love of music and sports, Laurel became a wonderful pal as well as a needed confidant for Mom. With her gift of clever repartee, ironic sense of humor, and knowledge of literature and Spanish, she enchanted Dad. With her innate openness and abundant charm, she won over my predictably more recalcitrant Grandma...despite being a Gentile.

My folks, Laurel, and I played lots of raucous team Scrabble, always the women against the men. The women usually won. Once, following one of our rare victories, Dad excused himself before the next game, then quietly returned. About halfway through the game, Laurel let out a "What?" Without fanfare, Dad had put on his special scarlet tie emblazoned with a dozen or so gray pigs, each mounted on the letters, MCP. Dad grinned impishly throughout the rest of the game, even as Mom and Laurel whomped us.

Laurel brought a new spark into my life and to family occasions. But there was something more. As fate would have it, her family, the Vermilyeas, would play an important role in my family relationships. When new, unresolvable tensions developed back in Kansas City, the Vermilyeas provided a special, strange, and unexpected refuge for my folks.

51

Cabo San Lucas

In March of 1979, a year after we got married, Mom, Dad, Laurel, and I took our only real trip together—four days in Cabo San Lucas at the southern tip of Baja, California. Grandma even felt good enough that Mom brought her out to Northern California to spend a month with Bob and Sylvia Lewis.

It was a wonderful getaway. We stayed at the old, original Cabo San Lucas Hotel, so isolated that it didn't even have a telephone, only radio communications. Dad and Mom seemed happier than ever, at least as viewed through my more mature eyes, not the rose-colored glasses of youth nor the cynical lenses of young adulthood.

Dad reveled in being back in Mexico, his *tierra*, admittedly a tierra observed from the vantage point of a lovely hotel. He talked for hours about what Mexico meant to him, taking special delight in sharing this with Laurel, with whom he could converse in his brain-surgery-reduced Spanish.

Dad appeared calmly self-fulfilled and content with his niche in life. Content with his enriched Mexican identity. His reconnection to California and his siblings. His somewhat illusory status in the Kansas Republican Party. His hypertrophied sense of being a Hispanic community leader. His continued service on national Boy Scout committees. And his pride in Gary's company presidency, especially since Gary generously asked for Dad's opinions, which Granddad had seldom done.

Mom, too, seemed unusually at ease. She talked about the new office atmosphere, now that she was a real team member with Gary and Dad, not the continuous (and futile) conflict mediator between Dad and Granddad. She appeared at reasonable peace with Gary and me. We would never be the exact kind of Jewish sons she would have sculpted, but she was happy with us. And she basked in the reflected pseudo-glory of attending events as the wife of Mr. Kansas Hispanic Republican.

It was great to see them so happy, so joyous...yes, so loving, nearly flirtatious. They held hands as they walked and even discussed holding a family reunion in Cabo.

About the only downside was that Dad tripped and fell several times. But, after all, he had never moved like Gene Kelly or Cary Grant. So Mom chided him, "Pick up your feet, Carlos. Don't shuffle. And you, too, Junior." As usual, Dad and I got a kick out of Mom's "You're-just-like-your-father" routine.

Then, early Saturday evening, the hotel received a radio message asking Mom to call Bob Lewis immediately. We caught a cab to the next hotel a couple of miles down the road, and Mom called Bob. The news wasn't good. Grandma had become ill. Mom had to go back up to Northern California instead of returning to Kansas City.

We were leaving the next day anyway, so the news didn't change our departure plans, but it did change the mood. We tried to comfort Mom. Even Dad consoled her, rubbing her back, putting his arm around her, and kissing her.

Our parting words blended encouragement for Mom, expressions of confidence about Grandma's condition, recollections of our wonderful four days, and, of course, discussion of a family reunion in Cabo. None of us realized that the family party was coming to an end.

52

Downhill

When Mom reached the Bay Area, she found Grandma worse off than we had imagined. She had life-threatening pancreatitis. Several weeks later, when Grandma was able to travel, Mom flew her back to Kansas City. Once home she bounced back physically, but not psychologically.

And while Dad's Cabo bruises healed, he didn't stop falling down. A diagnosis revealed that he had Parkinson's.

For Mom, the fleeting joy of Cabo liberation quickly turned into the recognition of her new, permanent, suffocating Kansas City reality—with a lonely, frightened mother and a rapidly declining husband. While continuing in the office, she also became the lifeline for these two needy, increasingly dependent people. Faced with these smothering pressures, the family rock began to crumble.

Grandma's growing dependence on Mom revealed itself in seemingly benign but ultimately corrosive ways. Since Granddad's death, Mom had called Grandma nearly every day and visited her regularly. But once a day no longer sufficed. Multiple phone calls were demanded. If Mom didn't stop by daily to see her on the way home from the office, she'd better have a damn good reason.

Every evening, once the last word had been uttered on the local ten p.m. TV newscast, Mom would call Grandma. When I was home, we would usually watch the newscast together, so I heard Mom's side of those calls. They usually had little to say, since they'd already talked several times that day. With failing eyesight, Grandma seldom read or went out, so she didn't have much new to add; Mom had to do most of the conversational heavy lifting. Yet Mom had to call every night at ten-thirty and promise to call her first thing the next morning. Mom had to adhere to the schedule, or else.

If Mom were a few minutes late in her nightly duty—she might have to go to the bathroom or be talking to someone else— Grandma would gently berate her. How worried she was that something had happened to Mom. How afraid she was that Mom had forgotten her (fat chance). Or, when she was in high dudgeon, how she had begun to doubt whether Mom still loved her. Mom would have to apologize, at length. I could see in Mom's face a growing resentment.

Then there was Dad. The stop-shuffling, pick-up-your-feet Carlos of Cabo San Lucas had become the stumbling, barely-able-to-pick-up-his-feet Carlos of Kansas City, with an accelerating loss of hearing, memory, and ability to communicate. On top of Dad's 1965 brain surgery and his long-term emphysema, Parkinson's was taking a terrible toll.

Years later I discovered a taped oral history interview with Dad in the Westside Branch of the Kansas City Public Library. His responses were slow, fumbling, and error laden. He got the year of his marriage wrong. He said that Gary (not me) lectured about bilingualism throughout the United States. He even referred to my daughter, Alana, as Carlotta (the name of one of his Mexican ancestors).

In the 1980 presidential primary season, Dad became one of the titular leaders of the George Bush for President campaign in Kansas. He had little good to say about Ronald Reagan, the other major Republican candidate. Reagan, however, made mincemeat of Bush in most of the early primaries. By the time of the Kansas state convention, it was merely a matter of choosing delegates who would vote for Reagan at the national convention.

Mom and Dad went, assuming Dad would be chosen as a delegate or alternate, as in 1972 and 1976. After all, according to Mom, Dad had earned so much respect from everyone in the party. Maybe so, but not enough to mollify the Reaganites. Unforgiving about Dad's early support for Bush, they rejected him. He also soon lost his state committee associate vice chairmanship.

Dad didn't say much, but it was clear that this rejection had deeply wounded this proud, sensitive, declining man. Mom went into tirades about how this was a personal insult after Dad's years of service to the party and the Hispanic community.

When Reagan chose Bush as his running mate, my folks sucked it up and pasted on Reagan-Bush bumper stickers, but they had little to do with the campaign. Dad's political run was over. As quickly as that, he had become a party has-been. So had Mom.

Grandma's and Dad's illnesses had dealt Mom a potent one-two punch. A lifetime's accumulation of blows was taking its toll, leaving Mom increasingly vulnerable to the slightest irritation. Maybe that's the best explanation I can give for her extreme reaction to an unintended punch from an unexpected place...from her favorite grandchild, Gary's oldest child, Rita.

Mom doted on Rita. She and Dad took her on trips to places they never took the other three grandchildren—to Yucatán,

Mexico, and to Spain to expose her to Dad's heritage. Mom had burst with pride during Rita's Bat Mitzvah, and for good reason. It was the best Mitzvah—Bat or Bar—I've ever attended. Rita's beautiful singing voice may have reminded Mom of her own when she was young—or at least her illusion of her former voice.

Then, during the summer of 1979 following her Bat Mitzvah, thirteen-year-old Rita attended Ramah, a Conservative Jewish summer camp in Wisconsin. Mom wasn't all that overjoyed. Even worse was what came out of Ramah. Upon returning home, Rita announced that she was going to keep kosher, something not even Gary and Debby were doing.

For Mom this was the proverbial straw that broke the camel's back. She had been hanging on by her fingernails. Rita's announcement pushed her over the edge. Dad tersely referred to it as "that kosher crap," but Mom went on the religious warpath.

Food became a major battleground. Mom would be damned if she was going to change her cooking habits when Gary's family came over for dinner. One of Rita's favorite dishes was spinach and cream cheese. So Mom would make it for her and then pointedly serve it alongside a meat dish, despite the kosher prohibition against mixing meat and dairy products. When Rita ate the spinach but refused to eat the meat, Mom would throw a fit.

After Ramah, the kosher factor transformed family dinners into mini-melodramas. It also undermined Mom's tenuous accommodation to the Conservative tack of Gary's Judaism. And it heightened another tension, this one of longer standing—the celebration of the December holiday season.

For Mom and Dad, this meant Christmas. For Gary, Debby, and their family, it meant Hanukkah. Mom and Dad viewed this as the rejection of a family tradition.

Over the years, Mom had told me how she had grown to hate the Christmas season because it meant loneliness, the absence of family, and the inability to greet her loved ones with the cherished "Merry Christmas." Rita's very personal and perfectly reasonable kosher decision had turned the arrival of Christmas into an existential nightmare for my folks.

I suggested that Mom and Dad spend the holidays with us. This included Christmas Day with Laurel's family, the Vermilyeas. For my folks this brought a burst, albeit a far too brief burst, of happy Decembers.

REARRANGEMENTS

53

Vermilyea Christmases

Laurel came from a huge, easy-going, all-embracing family. She and her seven siblings were raised just four blocks from the beach in Carlsbad, California, about thirty-five miles up the coast from San Diego.

Laurel's folks, transplanted midwesterners, had moved to Carlsbad during World War II. Her mother, Natalie, was Carlsbad's first police officer. Her father, Veblen, a semi-retired cowboy, returned periodically to Wyoming to ride the range.

The Vermilyeas owned two single-story homes connected by a joint patio, perfect for parties in the predictably lovely Southern California weather. Every Vermilyea family gathering brought a different mix. Brothers, sisters, sons, daughters, uncles, aunts, nieces, nephews, cousins, spouses, ex-spouses, and close friends might show up. With dozens of people arriving and leaving throughout the day, comings and goings were inconsistently acknowledged. It was up to you to make your own way, introduce yourself, join conversations, and try to keep track of participants without a scorecard.

Meals were semi-planned potluck affairs, with the emphasis on luck. With so many people involved and guest lists truly guess lists, perfect culinary balance was out of the question. They almost always ran out of mashed potatoes and salad before everybody sampled them, but usually had an excess of meat and desserts. It was chaos—wonderful, casual, joyous chaos.

Vermilyea Christmases, in particular, provided my folks with an escape from the frustration of not having full family Christmases in Kansas City. So they quickly fell in love with Decembers at the Vermilyeas.

At first my folks experienced culture shock from the Vermilyea anarchy, so different from the staid, orderly, and generally routine Kansas City family gatherings. But they soon adjusted, in differing fashions.

Mom's outgoing nature served her well. She drew on her facility with small talk, her eagerness to express opinions on just about everything, and her ability to wedge her way into conversations. Before long Mom was in her element (and the weather was mild, so she could smoke outside, a Vermilyea requirement).

Dad's sense of restraint tended to make him diffident in large groups of strangers. But he soon found a comrade in arms—Veb Vermilyea, Laurel's father, an open, honest, congenial, slow-talking man of few words. Although they had few real interests in common and although years of education separated them, they were drawn to each other. Dad saw in Veb someone who had lived part of Dad's dream—being a scion of the land, a wanderer, a man on horseback. Dad even talked to him about Cold Stream, his ex–polo pony that he had barely been able to ride. It was a meeting of spirits more than minds.

In the Vermilyeas, Mom and Dad found a huge, accepting, chaotic surrogate family, the kind of family each of them lacked—Mom, an only child; Dad, thousands of miles from his uncommunicative siblings. And in the Vermilyeas, nobody kept kosher.

54

Natalie's Bat Mitzvah

"Uncle Carlos, would you be willing to give one of the Torah blessings at my Bat Mitzvah?"

That telephone question—from Natalie, my brother Gary's middle child—sounded so simple. Later I learned that it emerged from lengthy family discussions about my appropriateness, considering my non-religious proclivities.

My answer was yes. My niece wanted me to give a blessing, so I would. In Hebrew.

Natalie sent me the written phonetic blessing so I could learn to say it properly. She also sent me a taped version of the chant. Well, why read when you get the opportunity to chant? So I memorized and practiced it, over and over and over.

But there was a catch. To give the blessing, I had to be called to the pulpit by my Hebrew name, which I didn't have. Carlos Eliseo Cortés didn't cut it.

According to Jewish tradition, if you don't have a Hebrew name, you start from scratch with the surname ben Avraham, meaning son of Abraham, the father of all Jews. I also needed a first name; Gary had already dubbed himself Gedaliah. Perusing a Hebrew name book, Laurel lit up. "I've got it! Barak, the Hebrew word for lightning. It's perfect." Perfect because the Corteses are among the slowest-moving people on earth. Why hurry when you don't need to?

So Barak ben Avraham, his wife, Laurel Cortés (I didn't ask her to change her name), and his daughter, Alana Cortés, headed back to Kansas City in February 1981.

Come the Bat Mitzvah, the various blessing givers before me simply read from a phonetically spelled card sitting by the open Torah. For a moment I considered following the crowd. But after all of my practice? So when my turn came, I chanted. Barak ben Avraham, not Carlos Cortés.

From the moment I stepped behind the pulpit, something took over. I chanted beautifully, fluidly, sonorously. Afterward numerous people made a point of telling me how special my chant had been.

But there was something else. For the first and maybe only time in my life I felt truly spiritual. I felt the presence of…well, let's just leave it at that.

Although I chanted the blessing three more times at Bar Mitzvahs of members of our extended family, that feeling never returned. But Barak ben Avraham had become another part of my multicultural self.

* * *

Natalie's Bat Mitzvah would have been memorable to me just because of the blessing. But that weekend also revealed that family stresses were wreaking havoc on Mom.

Mom had stalwartly shouldered the increasing pressures of Dad's rapidly progressing Parkinson's and emphysema. But she had gone ballistic about Gary's family's lurch into kosher-keeping and ever more Conservative Judaism. Then there was Grandma— lonely, fearful, increasingly dependent Grandma.

On Friday night, Bat Mitzvah eve, family and friends dribbled into town, so Gary and Debby held a dinner for out-of-towners at the Woodside Racket Club.

The room was small and cramped. Three tables in a long U-shaped setup, with everyone sitting around the outside, facing nobody. I ended up next to one of Gary's friends who taught at some midwestern university. Mom, who hadn't seen me since Christmas, also sat with us. Grandma ended up across the room on the opposite leg of the U with one of her nieces.

As Laurel and I left the dinner, we heard a horrendous wailing in the lobby. It was Grandma, moaning and emoting, "I never thought I would see the day when my own daughter would refuse to sit with me at dinner!"

Taken aback, poor Mom tried to explain to her, in front of an audience of thousands (make that forty), that the two of them just happened to end up at different parts of the table. She hadn't seen me for two months. She hadn't intentionally avoided sitting with her. Unfazed, Grandma wailed all the way to the car.

Mom was crestfallen. Publicly mortified. Ridden with guilt. Sincerely worried about Grandma. She drove Grandma back to her apartment, apologizing all the way. As soon as we got home she called her with more apologies, but Grandma wouldn't accept them, lift the guilt, and give Mom a good night's sleep.

Mom had been a devoted, caring, loving, attentive, self-sacrificing daughter. Grandma couldn't have asked for anything more. But she did.

When Mom hung up the phone, her eyes betrayed her. They yearned for freedom...freedom from the accumulation of pressures that were pushing her toward the breaking point.

THE SHORT GOODBYE

55

Mom Dies

Freedom never came. Cancer got there first.

For several months Mom had been feeling heavy congestion in her chest. Shortly after Thanksgiving 1982, the doctor ran some tests. It was lung cancer.

When Mom called, she told me not to worry, that she was going to lick it. But I'd heard that tone of voice and those fighting words before. Like when she had received the anonymous Beth El letter about her singing, vowed not to quit, yet never again sang publicly.

None of the courage, determination, and stamina Mom exhibited when doing business or supporting other family members seemed to translate into matters concerning herself. The relentless daily family grind had worn her down. Mom didn't have much fight left in her. Every few days I would hear those same words of resolve cloaked in the voice of surrender.

Mom decided to go to the M. D. Anderson Cancer Clinic in Houston, but she couldn't get an appointment until shortly before Christmas. I flew to Houston to meet Mom and Dad, who had rented a two-bedroom suite in an apartment hotel directly across the street from the hospital. When Dad opened the door, he put his arms around me and said brokenly, "I'm really glad you're here, Carlos. Your mother's not doing very well."

Mom's weakening phone voice should have given me ample warning, but I hadn't lost the vision of my robust, strong-striding, firm-speaking mother. So I was unprepared for this frail, quaking stranger. Stretched out on the couch. Barely able to sit up. Unable to get to the bathroom without help.

Dad, too, was barely recognizable. Even as his Parkinson's had steadily sapped his powerful body, he had maintained his spunk. But no longer. Dad's eyes cried out for help.

I did what I could. The next day meant endless forms and hours of waiting, interrupted occasionally by blood tests and X-rays. Talkative Mom had become a silent heap, slumped in her wheelchair, shivering in her hospital gown. Dad had downshifted from short answers to yes's and no's. I tried to make conversation, knowing it would draw little response.

Finally, in the late afternoon, we saw the assigned oncologist. Without preliminaries, he read Mom's file, quickly surveyed the X-rays, and abruptly asked her, "How long have you smoked?"

Mom's barely audible "about fifty years" quickly earned a second question, "How much?" "Half a pack a day" (understatement). By now the doctor was punching his calculator to ascertain the precise chemotherapy treatment. "Well, you've got cancer" (surprise!) and "we'd better start treatment right away" (meaning today).

The inevitable came as a sudden jolt. It was like hearing "curtain going up" before you've finished putting on your costume and makeup. Everything unfolded with startling rapidity after a long, punishing day of bone-chilling delay. The official battle for Mom's life had begun.

A nurse rolled Mom into the chemotherapy room—deep, narrow, barren, congested. Against two long parallel walls sat dozens of beds, each containing a prone, staring, moaning, puking patient, passively receiving whatever medicines dripped out of plastic bags through needles into veins. Within seconds Mom was added to the line of inert sufferers. I thanked God that Grandma and Granddad weren't there to witness it. After the treatment, Dad and I took Mom back to the hotel on the shuttle van.

Thus began my Christmas vacation. We made trips back and forth between the hotel and the hospital for chemotherapy, each visit a struggle to get Mom and Dad in and out of the van. As we watched New Year's Day football games with Mom lying in the next room, Dad could hardly make sense of the action.

When I headed back to California for the beginning of the winter quarter, Gary flew down to take my place. But just for a week. He, too, had to get back to work. With Dad gone, he *was* the construction company.

Once Gary returned to Kansas City, Dad was on his own. So it came as little surprise when, a few days later, I got his terrified call that Mom had taken a turn for the worse. Gary and I flew back to Houston. Mom was now in the intensive care ward, but her condition had stabilized and the ward doctor said that as soon as she got a little better she could return to outpatient status at the hotel.

Chemo may or may not have been helping Mom, but the stay in Houston was killing Dad. It didn't take Gary and me long to come to the obvious decision. Shortly after Mom's release from intensive care, we transferred them back to Kansas City, where Mom could live at home and be treated by a local oncologist, while Dad could recover in his own familiar environment.

Mom spiraled downward, punctuated by interludes of stability. During a few brief, hope-raising upward blips, she would sit up, occasionally do word puzzles, even go out to dinner, usually at Gary and Debby's house. When the Carlos F. Cortés Health Lodge was dedicated that summer at Boy Scout Camp Osceola,

Mom was too sick to attend. But she managed to go down to the office for a brief ceremony, specially arranged so she could be there.

I spent much of summer 1983 in Kansas City, helping Mom, buoying up Dad, and giving a modicum of relief to Debby and Gary, who now had to care for three dependent adults while also raising three kids and running a business.

When Laurel and I flew back to Kansas City for Thanksgiving, Mom had turned into a comatose bag of bones. She almost never left her bed and had become dependent on full-time nursing care. I visited her bedroom regularly throughout the weekend, but she lacked the energy—or the will—to converse. I prattled on about this and that, with little reaction. Laurel may have gotten the biggest response when, on Saturday, Mom summoned up the energy to whisper to her, "It's hard. It's *so* hard."

But that weekend wasn't just about Mom. It was also about our family.

With life oozing out of her, Mom turned against Grandma. When we would go back to the bedroom together, Mom would glare at Grandma, a look that blended love and fury, affection and frustration. It was an "I'll never get to spend one day of my life free of you" look.

Always the devoted daughter, during the ten years since Granddad's death Mom had dedicated herself to comforting and supporting her mother. Now Mom was dying *before* Grandma. She would never know what it would be like not to have to call Grandma four times a day, visit her constantly, shepherd her around, cajole her when she was depressed, and suffer Grandma's barbs when Mom made even the slightest miscue.

Late on Saturday afternoon, a crestfallen Grandma came back from the bedroom. "My daughter doesn't want to talk to me any more," she said. I consoled her, telling her this wasn't true, that Mom was just having a bad day. But I knew it was true...and why. I'm afraid Grandma did, too.

Laurel and I returned to California on Sunday. That Thursday I received another call from Gary. Mom had been rushed to the hospital. If we wanted to see her again before she died, we'd better come right away.

So on Friday, December 2, Laurel, Alana, and I headed back to Kansas City. Debby met us at the airport and took us to pick up Dad on the way to the hospital. As we walked into the house the phone was ringing. A few moments later Dad came out of his study.

"Your mother just died."

56

Mom's Long Shadow

Nothing about Mom's burial came easy. Not the casket. Not the funeral service. Especially not the burial site.

The night Mom died, Dad seemed more alone than I could remember. Mom—even the comatose companion of the past year—was gone. Gary and I weren't enough. He wanted his brothers around him in his time of need (Susie had died and Elena was living in distant Puerto Vallarta).

Dad called Vinnie, Alex, and Eduardo, telling them that Mom had died and asking them—no, begging them—to join him for the funeral. Dad hadn't spoken to Vinnie for more than a decade, so it came as no surprise when he declined. So did Alex, with whom Dad almost never talked. Only Eduardo came, with his wife, Jean.

The next day Gary and I took Dad to Stine & McClure Funeral Home, where we helped him choose the appropriate casket and make the rest of the logistical arrangements. When it came to open or closed casket, Dad was adamant—closed. Nobody at the funeral was going to see the gaunt remains of his wife. They were going to remember the trim, healthy, vigorous Florence Cortés.

Then there was the issue of the funeral service, especially the eulogy. Although Mom had refused to return to Temple B'nai Jehudah, Gary had maintained his membership even as he became active in Conservative Synagogue Beth Shalom. Gary arranged for B'nai Jehudah rabbi Michael Zedek to conduct the service. He barely knew Mom, so on Saturday evening he came over to Gary's house to talk about her with the family.

We talked and talked and talked. Dad and Grandma. Gary and I. Laurel and Debby. Ed and Jean. My daughter, Alana. Gary's kids—Rita, Natalie, and Marc.

The evening started slowly and solemnly while the rabbi took notes. Soon, Florence stories began to flow, some funny, some sad, most ironic—Mom's strengths and foibles, her successes and excesses, her excellence and eccentricities. We laid Mom out, warts and all, for the rabbi. Dad capped it off in semi-privacy. As the rabbi was leaving, with only Laurel standing within earshot, Dad pulled him aside and said, matter-of-factly, "Let's face it, Rabbi, she was a heller."

Then there was the issue of the burial site. Grandma and Granddad had set up a sort of family plot at Rose Hill, Temple B'nai Jehudah's cemetery. Granddad was already there, along with other relatives. There were spaces for Grandma and for Mom. But not for Dad. To memorialize his love for the Boy Scouts and his antipathy for all organized religion, Dad had added a codicil to his will—a sardonic, typically Cortés codicil:

I desire that I be given no formal funeral service, but in lieu thereof a brief five-minute service shall be had by each religious faith with which the various members of my family shall then be affiliated.

After that his body was to be cremated and his ashes strewn from an airplane over his beloved Boy Scout Camp Osceola.

But as cancer shriveled her body, Mom became, well, I guess the word is desperate. She begged Dad not to be cremated, but to be buried next to her. And she prevailed.

Dad, however, insisted on one non-negotiable proviso. He was damned if he'd be buried anywhere near—and I can still hear his snarl—anywhere near "that son of a bitch Morris Hoffman." More than ten years after Granddad's death, Dad still wanted revenge. Even in her final days, Mom couldn't avoid being the family battlefield. Forced for the last time to choose sides, she chose Dad.

Gary and I took Dad out to Rose Hill, where we picked two adjoining grave sites. But we didn't decide who would tell Grandma that Mom was not going to be buried next to her and Granddad. I think Gary and I both just sort of hoped the other would do it. Nobody did.

Then came the funeral.

After our Saturday evening meeting with Rabbi Zedek, filled with disparate musings, we all had the same question. What is he going to say about Mom? Well, miracles do happen. His eulogy was a masterpiece.

Florence Cortés was a woman of distinction and strength. A lady with charm and assertiveness, of influence and skill.

Those qualities and more were apparent in every aspect of her too few years. For her life was of one cloth. She cared deeply, intensely about all she did. Were it not so, she simply wouldn't do it: From extraordinary business skill to a fundamental commitment to the fine arts; to her own singing and piano; to a host of volunteer organizations; to her ceaseless devotion to her beloved mother, her husband, her children and grandchildren.

Florence's devotion came with an intensity which sets her apart from the tepid, the insecure, or insincere. One knew of her opinion and her caring every step of the way. Hand in hand with that concern came a sense of precision, a desire to do the job the right way. For she was a perfectionist who if she assumed a responsibility, one could count the task as done and done with unmatched quality....

That is why the fifty years of strength shared with her Carlos saw them as husband and wife, partners, as supporters of each other's interests, and as friends. The passing years only enhanced their regard, for they were committed to each other by a contract—as Carlos called it—'a contract of the heart.'

That is why she shaped in substantial manner the character and devotion of her sons, Carlos and Gary. Her concern for their families, her four grandchildren. That is why their lives remain fully involved with hers as well. And, of course, the daily and precious links to her mother, Ada.

For to be part of her life meant you got all of her life. Her opinions, her beliefs, her devotion, respect, concern, her love. And that is why we must recognize, celebrate that for seventy-one years we were part of a miracle. A unique and special human being—alas, her physical presence is no more. But she is part of us still. Amen.

Rabbi Zedek had made Mom live this one last time. Not an artificial, polished, purified, perfect Mom, but the real, unvarnished, opinionated, perfectionist Mom, whose sometimes irritating words and actions often obscured the woman we all loved and admired. The rabbi had returned her to us.

* * *

It would be nice to end on this high note. But an even more intense moment—the burial—lay just around the corner.

As the limousine headed from the funeral home to the cemetery, Grandma was already stunned because of the closed-casket service. She had expected to get one last look at her daughter, but Dad's decision had denied her that opportunity.

When we entered the cemetery and began the circular drive among the graves, Grandma was in a trance. Suddenly she burst into shocked awareness. "Why are we going past our family plot?" Silence from those who didn't know what was going on and from Gary and me, who knew all too well. "But we passed Florence's grave!"

The procession stopped, and the disgorging of occupants, living and dead, began. Gary and I led our disbelieving grandmother over the frozen turf to Mom's hole in the ground. When the horror of the situation finally hit her, this tiny, elegant woman sprang into action, hopeless action, trying to stop the inevitable. "What's happening? There must be some mistake. My daughter can't be buried here. Next to her father and me she's supposed to be."

Gary and I did our best to comfort her. "But Grandma, Carlos and I chose this plot because...because it's near the rose garden, and you know how much Mom loved roses. And look, Granddad's just across the driveway where he can see her." We were as comforting as a bed of spikes.

I glanced at Dad. He had never looked more Mexican. Despondent, triumphant, inscrutable. But his stoic face masked what must have been a terrible internal struggle: the grief over Mom's death doing battle with the exhilaration of triumph over the Hoffmans.

* * *

The next time I visited Kansas City I went out to Rose Hill, alone. There I saw—clearly and starkly—the reality behind Grandma's funeral wailing. Mom wasn't buried just across the driveway where Granddad could see her, as we had assured Grandma. She was buried seventy-five yards away! I paced it myself. Dad had seen to it that neither he nor Mom would be buried within shouting distance of her father.

Then there was Mom's gravestone—Florence H. Cortés. Not Florence Hoffman Cortés, as Mom usually referred to herself. Instead, Hoffman had been reduced to a terse, anonymous *H.*

Dad had gotten in the last word. After fifty years of struggle with Granddad for emotional supremacy in Mom's eyes, Dad had made certain that Mom would rest for eternity as Carlos Cortés's wife, not as Morris Hoffman's daughter.

57

Dad's Last Hurrah

Mom's death seemed to exorcise Dad's demons. He became more mellow. And he and Grandma became friends. I mean real friends. At family dinners, the two of them would sit together, alone, reminiscing about old times in a way I'd never seen before.

More amazing was the way Dad now talked about Granddad. Sometimes he even referred to him by his first name, Morris. Not like in the past, when it was "your Grandfather," at best, and scatological language when he was angry. Just Morris, plain old Morris, as if they'd been great buddies.

It was as if Mom's burial had cleaned the slate...and more. In those last days, Grandma finally seemed to realize that this strange—to her—this strange Mexican had brought happiness to her captivating but sometimes irascible daughter. And Dad, so physically isolated from his uncommunicative California Mexican siblings, finally seemed to realize that these two strange—to him—these strange Jewish immigrants had given him something he desperately wanted, a tangible sense of family.

For a time after Mom's death, Dad tried to get by in his huge, rambling, empty home. But as days passed, its enormity reinforced his loneliness.

Add Dad's growing difficulty in getting around. Driving was becoming increasingly perilous. He had trouble parking, sometimes drove up on the curb, and once got himself so lodged into a parking space that he had to call for help to get out of the car. Gary and I soon concluded that we had to get rid of Dad's car before he killed himself or somebody else. Gary did the dirty duty.

This hastened the inevitable. Isolated in the suburbs with no car, increasingly accident prone, and far from public transportation, Dad was virtually helpless. We finally convinced him that he needed to move.

Gary and I set him up in the Villa Ventura, a nice seniors' complex in a semi-rural southern section of Kansas City. Dad rented a three-bedroom corner apartment, transforming one bedroom into a study and keeping a guest bedroom so I could stay with him during my Kansas City visits. Gary and Debby bought Dad's house.

I visited Dad about once a month, always staying in his apartment, eating most of my meals in the Villa Ventura dining room, and meeting his many new friends, in particular, women. The Villa Ventura's enormous gender imbalance had helped make Dad a sought-after companion.

Dad also returned to his religious roots. One of the other residents was a charming Catholic priest who connected with Dad through both faith and intellect. The priest conducted brief daily ecumenical services and held Mass on Sunday. Dad attended regularly, went to confession, and began taking communion.

But there was one more important loose end—Dad's brother, Vinnie, in California. The two hadn't spoken for more than a decade, except for Dad's futile call asking Vinnie to come to Mom's funeral. So Vinnie's oldest son, Dick, and I decided to try to bring them together. Like two minor court officials attempting to patch up some medieval dispute between estranged members of the royal family, Dick and I negotiated with the two highnesses and arranged for a meeting.

Dad was coming out to California for a national Boy Scout leadership conference in San Diego. Afterward Laurel and I drove him out to Indian Wells, where Vinnie spent most weekends in his comfortable second home in a gated golfing community. There we gathered—Vinnie and family along with Dad, Laurel, and me.

We talked, ate, drank, swam, and even took a family photo, which I've never seen. A pleasant but unremarkable weekend. I had hoped that Dad and Vinnie would unearth interesting family tidbits for my collection of Cortés lore, but it didn't happen.

During our drive to Indian Wells, Dad kept repeating how he and Vinnie had lots to talk about since they hadn't seen each other for so long. Yet they said little of substance.

Dick, Laurel, and I decided that maybe having the whole family around was inhibiting them, that they needed some time alone. So on the last afternoon we all went into the backyard to swim and picnic, leaving the two patriarchs to have some precious one-on-one time in the living room.

A couple of hours later, Laurel and I decided to peek in to see how things were going. They weren't. There they sat, on opposite sides of the small living room, two fat old Mexicans staring silently at each other. Neither having energy, interest, or initiative to propel the conversation. Both excruciatingly aware how much opportunity they had squandered with their ridiculous feud, but unable to say or do anything to eradicate its effects.

On the way back to Riverside, Dad said little about their reunion except the obligatory remarks about having had a good time. In fact, Dad didn't say much at all during the ride. Maybe he had finally come to grips with the realization of his loss. That a family tree, no matter how laden with names and interesting ancestors, does not equal a family. And maybe this helped him appreciate more fully what Grandma and Granddad Hoffman had given him, in their own peculiar way.

*   *   *

Dad and Vinnie never saw each other again. Dick and I talked about planning a family reunion and starting a family newsletter. Both might have happened if Dad had stuck around a bit longer. But his time was growing short.

Dad's next California trip came in December 1984 so he could spend his cherished Christmas with Laurel's family. To bring him out, I flew back to Kansas City, where I found him at the height of his new Villa Ventura social life, with parties nearly every night. But socializing was also taking its toll. Dad planned to spend a month in California—first with us, then at the Vermilyeas for Christmas, and finally up north with Eduardo and Alex. But from the time we got off the plane he began acting strangely.

At dinner out one night, he disappeared. I was about ready to call the police when here came Dad, out of the *women's* restroom!

When I helped Dad unpack in his beachfront hotel in Carlsbad, I found his suitcase loaded with odd and sundry items from our house—coasters, silverware, statuettes. Dad didn't even seem to notice their presence.

The night after the Vermilyea Christmas party, I got a call from the hotel that Dad wasn't feeling good. I rushed over, followed shortly by the paramedics, who took him to the nearby hospital for observation. The next day the doctor determined that Dad had suffered oxygen deprivation during the flight, heightening the effect of his Parkinson's and emphysema. Worse yet, being away from his familiar surroundings had totally disoriented him. The doctor urged me to get Dad home, quickly, even if it meant flying. Dad's plans to go up north to see Eduardo and Alex would have to be put on hold...for good, it turned out.

Ontario (California) Airport, from where we flew, was still in the horse-and-buggy days, with no indoor ramps to the planes. Passengers had to climb up portable stairs from the runway. Dad couldn't make it. Instead they had to use a lift.

It was heartbreaking. Dad, seated in a wheelchair, staring straight ahead as he was raised up to the cabin door in full view of everyone. It must have been crushing to this proud, dignified, intensely private man. And Dad probably realized that he was seeing California, land of his birth, for the last time.

I spent the rest of Christmas vacation at Dad's apartment. Gone was his riotous joy of a week earlier. I wheeled him to meals and to his few visits with friends. And he hardly talked to me. Once, as I was watching a college football game, he cursorily asked me, "Is it the Super Bowl yet?"

Throughout the next year I visited Kansas City often. Dad had good days and bad ones. At times he was able to take short walks outside. He resumed his social life, although less frenetically. Occasionally Gary would take Dad down to the office, but there was nothing for him to do except try to read the *Wall Street Journal* and look through stacks of old plans.

Sometimes Dad actually seemed eager to work on projects, unlike Mom, who had surrendered to living death the moment she learned of her cancer. At times he and I would talk about the family history he had long dreamed of writing, although we didn't make much headway. We translated a few old Spanish letters and tried to identify now-unfamiliar faces in his collection of old Mexican family photos.

Other times, Dad reminisced about politics. I helped him compose a letter to his friend Senator Robert Dole of Kansas, encouraging him to run for president in 1988 and offering to coordinate the Hispanics for Dole Campaign. Obviously this would be impossible given Dad's condition, but he felt good sending the letter.

God bless Bob Dole. He responded with a warm, personal letter saying that he was weighing his options and would contact Dad once he had made a decision. To the end Dad talked about how he was looking forward to organizing Hispanics for Dole.

58

End of the Line

In August 1985, less than two years after Mom, Grandma died. Dad cried at her funeral.

Not long after Grandma's death, Dad's decline accelerated. Barely able to converse or to hear, and having difficulty breathing, he had to be moved to the next-door nursing facility. Later he entered the hospital, for good.

Because of the hospital affiliations of their respective doctors, the last days of my family members contained an ironic note of religious border-crossing. Granddad had died in the Episcopalian

St. Luke's Hospital, while Mom and Grandma had died in the Baptist Medical Center. Dad spent his last days in Menorah, a Jewish hospital.

Force of will kept him going for a while, but the accumulation of maladies was too much. The end came on December 14, 1985. The *Kansas City Star* ran a sixteen-inch-long obituary complete with a photo and a two-column headline, "Carlos F. Cortes, 78, Hispanic leader, dies."

For the last time, Gary called with the bad news. Laurel, Alana, and I flew back for our third funeral in two years. Everything seemed to operate on autopilot—the arrangements at the funeral home, the ceremony, the drive to Rose Hill Cemetery, the burial, the mourning receptions, and the tears, although there weren't many left.

Within two years I had lost Mom, then Grandma, then finally Dad. When August 1985 began, I was part of our family's third generation. In less than four months, Grandma's and Dad's deaths had erased two generations and made me, at fifty-one, the senior member of our family.

There was one final irony. Dad, who had written a codicil insisting that he wanted no formal funeral ceremony, ended up with two—first a Jewish service before his burial at Rose Hill, then a Catholic Mass.

Four days after the funeral, Dad's priest at the Villa Ventura conducted a commemorative Mass in his honor. Laurel and Alana had gone back to California. I went out alone and had to stand in the hallway. The place was packed. The priest conducted a profoundly moving ceremony. Tears flowed freely, far more than at Dad's official service.

Afterward, his friends insisted on talking to me, for hours. Story after story eulogized Dad—his gentility, his kindness, his warmth, his charm, his wit, his thoughtfulness, his personality. His agile mind? His quick intellect? His great memory?

Was this the man our family had been watching for twenty years, ever since his brain surgery? Stumbling, falling apart physically, struggling with his memory, constantly frustrated when he couldn't find the right words?

No, these old people had spotted someone our family's eyes could no longer see—that special man, the man who had raised me. That dislocated sixteenth-century Mexican aristocrat who somehow or other got trapped in the wrong time and place. The Dad who would take me to boxing matches and then spend the evening talking to me about ethics, honor, values, and chivalry. The man who would find a lonely teenager in his bedroom, drop everything, and then read and talk to me for hours, sometimes whole weekends, about literature—Hugo, Dickens, Melville, and, of course, Cervantes.

Yet all the time realizing that he'd have to pay a stiff price for his actions, that he'd probably catch hell from Granddad for not visiting some job or finishing a report. Because Granddad wouldn't understand—couldn't be expected to understand—how precious those hours were for Dad. And how absolutely vital they were for me.

It wasn't until that day in the Villa Ventura that I finally realized what a truly lucky little guy I had been. When I left the Villa Ventura that day—or evening—it was as if an enormous weight had been lifted from my shoulders. The weight of memories. The weight of family conflict. The weight of Kansas City.

59

Love Letters

There's one more twist.

One afternoon, after I had begun writing this story, Laurel suggested that I look at a huge box of letters sitting in our garage. I vaguely remembered them. Back when she was in high school,

Alana had brought over a box her mother had run across in her (formerly our) garage. It was full of bundles of letters that I had written to my folks from various stops in my life—New York; Brazil; Stratford, Connecticut; Fort Gordon, Georgia. I quickly glanced at the box, then stuck it in our garage.

When I casually responded that I'd get around to the letters when I had time, Laurel became uncharacteristically insistent. "I think you ought to look at them right now. The top letter is post-marked 1933."

1933? I wasn't even *born* until 1934. 1933 was the year my folks got married.

I found the letters, all in envelopes, bound by a string. The top letter was addressed to Miss Florence Hoffman, 3716 Benton Boulevard, Kansas City, Missouri. The postmark read May 17, 1933, Oakland, California. It was from Dad to Mom. The other forty-eight letters were meticulously organized in chronological order, ending in early July.

Dad wrote the first letter on May 17, the day Mom and Grandma got on the train from California to Kansas City after Mom's graduation from Cal. That same night Dad wrote, "I am writing to you again today so that you will be sure to get a letter from me every day and so that I may tell you what is in my heart." And the next day: "I am going to try to go for you as soon as possible. Your being away from me is more than I can endure." And the day after that. Sometimes twice a day. The last one was sent from Albuquerque on July 10 as Dad was heading to Kansas City for their wedding.

I didn't leave the couch until I had finished all of the letters. They were informative, revealing, sometimes heartbreaking, yet also frustrating. Frustrating because they referred to things I couldn't fully understand, asked questions for which there were no written answers, and responded to words that I couldn't read. Unless...

I ran back to the box. Was it too much to hope for? There, at the bottom of the box, covered and concealed for who knows how long, was another stack, Mom's letters to Dad. Once again neatly tied, but not nearly so nicely assembled—some in envelopes, some loose, not all dated.

The first letter was addressed to Mr. Carlos F. Cortés, 123 Tamalpais Road, Berkeley, California, and postmarked May 18, 1933, Barstow, California—obviously deposited by Mom during one of the train's cross-country stops. "I sat here and cried for quite a while," she wrote. Mom also sent letters, reflecting her changing moods, from Albuquerque ("I'm simply miserable. I haven't been so train sick in all the time I've been traveling on trains.") and from Newton, Kansas ("I haven't much to say as the trip is so terribly dull."), before she started sending letters from Kansas City.

Dad's letters chased Mom across the country in pursuing trains, finally catching up with her after she got home. Mom's letters didn't arrive in Berkeley until after Dad had written several himself.

No cell phones or e-mail then. Just two lonely people writing letters into space, prisoners of postal workers, train schedules, and geography, expressing love, emitting anguished cries, and voicing questions of concern, knowing they wouldn't receive answers for at least a week. But how did those letters end up in my garage? I tried to reconstruct their journey.

In her fastidious way, I can see super-organized Mom folding each of Dad's letters, replacing it in its original envelope, carefully storing them in chronological order, and later tying them in a bundle. Less methodical Dad, on the other hand, probably put some of them back in their envelopes (often the wrong envelopes, I discovered) and sometimes discarded the envelopes. He probably tossed them all—letters and envelopes—into some drawer or box. Later, Mom tried to reassemble the letters in chronological order, although not all were dated. I can even hear her sniping at Dad for being lackadaisical and Dad responding with a shrug of disgust or burst of ire. Having completed her impossible task as best she could, she had bundled Dad's letters.

The letters most likely traveled with them: to Berkeley; Kansas City; Lawrence, Kansas; back to Kansas City; then out south to our first home on Rockhill and Oak; and finally over to their dream house in Shawnee-Mission, Kansas.

I can remember seeing the letters only once, on a sweltering Kansas City evening in the summer of '54 when Mom was having one of her exceptionally bad nights during their separation, a night so bad that she furiously attacked her memory cabinet.

With me as sole witness, Mom ripped up part of her wedding dress. Then she cut Dad's face out of their wedding pictures. Finally, she pulled out the two bundles of letters, shook them at me, and shouted, "The great love affair! This is all that's left of it."

She was about to destroy them, but I asked her to give them to me. She threw them at me instead. I took them back to my bedroom and dropped them into one of my dresser drawers. I probably planned to read them later, but with the summer's chaos, I never got around to it. In fact, I forgot all about them, as did Mom and Dad.

The letters must have sat there for fourteen years, buried under whatever else I put on top of them. Then, in December 1968 when I returned from Brazil and shipped my stuff out to Riverside, I probably dumped everything from my drawers into big packing boxes. This included hundreds of my letters that Mom had carefully saved for me, and, unknowingly, Dad's and Mom's letters to each other.

In California they sat for another fifteen years among dozens of other boxes in my first house's garage until my ex-wife, Murielle, discovered them and asked Alana to bring them over to my home. I probably saw my own letters on top, assumed they were all from me, and consigned them to my garage for another decade or so… until the day Laurel decided to reorganize the garage. Not content with the letters on top, she dug a little deeper.

I shudder when I think of the decades when those letters could have been lost, discarded, destroyed by rain, or gnawed by varmints. But they survived. Maybe they were destined to survive.

Now, at the very time I was trying to reconstruct our family's story, the letters had been revealed to me. And as I read them, I yet again rediscovered my family, as I had so many times before.

The letters told the story of two people who were truly in love. Their love leaped from the pages, but in different ways. Dad wrote with passion ("I absolutely must have you if I must go on living.") and expressions of dreams ("We must accomplish something out of our married life and not just allow ourselves to slump."). Mom also wrote with love ("I want to get out in some wide open spaces and scream for you."), but blended this, sometimes jarringly, with complaints and self-pity ("I'm so tired that I could sit down and cry. I've been downtown all day shopping and I am just miserable.").

Over the weeks Mom's letters became more scripted than spontaneous, more demanding than understanding ("Louse, I didn't hear from you for the last 2 days. What's the big idea?"). And, as the wedding approached, they became more focused on details than feelings, since she, not Dad, was handling the logistics ("The chief trouble is with the bridesmaids. The dresses I pick out they don't like and the ones they pick out I don't like.").

Nowhere in the letters is there a reference to a phone conversation. In those ancient times, long-distance calls were a luxury ("I would like to call you but I can't afford it dearest."). While this may seem bizarre to contemporary readers accustomed to the instant gratification of 24/7 cyberspace connectedness, it appears as if they may never have talked in the nearly two months between Mom's departure from Berkeley and Dad's arrival in Kansas City a couple of days before the wedding.

Each letter contained urgent questions and pressing issues, but answers would not arrive for a week. This meant lots of drawn-out misunderstandings, especially involving religion (Dad wrote of "the accusing finger which will be pointed at us always saying, 'nothing good from intermarriage.' That will come from both sides.").

Of course, Grandma and Granddad Hoffman were not over-joyed about the wedding, regularly raising the issue of Dad's reli-gion. Forget the later rationalizations that Dad was "really Jew-ish" because of his mother. Mom's letters made it clear that her folks never bought into that rhetoric: "I haven't mentioned it to you before as I didn't believe it necessary. But whenever anyone has asked about you, the first question is 'Well, is he Jewish?' Naturally, I've said yes. And, too, although Dad is taking it like a good sport, still underneath he is a little hurt."

Dad understood, writing: "It is very hard for them to give you after so many years of your having been away. Besides to a stranger when they had hoped it might be a local boy. Also to a former Catholic when it should have been a Jewish boy. To a poor man, when it should have been a rich man. In all respects I am not the son-in-law that they wanted. I am sorry but I have done my best to please. I can't do more."

Once the decision had been made to get married in July, the letters became more argumentative, including about logistics. Consider their contrasting personal trajectories.

Dad was working full time at a gas station, taking an evening course in accounting, and looking for a place for them to live. You can feel Dad's fatigue and anxiety as he tried to find an apart-ment that would please Mom but was still affordable on his mea-ger salary ("I know that you love a fireplace so I am trying hard to find one that has one."). Yet despite trying to cut corners finan-cially, he still insisted on class, scolding Mom when the wedding announcements were sent without his full name, Carlos Federico Cortés ("It's really very much out of line not to have the groom's name printed in full as that is the future name of the bride.").

Mom, back in Kansas City, had become re-immersed in her pampered home life. Her letters were filled with apartment requirements that Dad simply could not meet—space, layout, view, location, furnishings. Each day spent in her nice Kansas City home inflated Mom's idea of what she needed to be happy.

Imagine Dad, returning from a day pumping gas, lubricating cars, and changing oil, then reading Mom's letters bitching about the Kansas City heat, lamenting her duties (hemming dish towels and learning how to darn socks), describing the oh-so-tiring round of showers and bridal parties (whose gifts she listed in detail), and elaborating on her expanding housing expectations ("Be sure that it has as nice a style as the one we saw. And I want a large living room. No cramped quarters for us, darling. We wouldn't be satisfied.").

Now imagine Mom's disappointment when Dad informed her that, given cost and availability, he had chosen a small one-room flat, a remodeled garage attic in the Berkeley hills. When she objected, he found another slightly larger bare-bones place ("I would like something more but we can't afford it.").

But the apartment disagreement paled next to the conflict over the wedding itself. From the pages erupted the battles that had become part of family lore, particularly the choosing of a best man and a wedding date.

There was the story of Dad's invitation to his Omaha Gentile friend, Paul Markham, to be his best man, an invitation he later rescinded. There were Mom's aggravating words: "Darling, I've decided on the date. It just dawned on me yesterday that my daddy's birthday is July 18th and I can't think of any more suitable date." But not for my Dad. He'd be damned if he would share his wedding date with Daddy!

Mom and Dad came up with their explosive suggestions about the same time. Their bombshell letters probably passed each other somewhere around Albuquerque.

And there was Mom's suggested compromise, which Dad accepted, the first of the many intermarriage compromises that would characterize their fifty years together and the turbulent multicultural world in which I grew up: "I'll compromise with you. I'll have the wedding on Sunday if you agree not to have Paul Markham for your best man. I told mother about him and just left her downstairs crying. She says that this is just one of the obstacles and disagreements which come up in intermarriage.... I haven't said anything to Dad as I know he'll blow up and there will be hell to pay and frankly, he isn't fully reconciled to the religious differences."

As I reread the letters—and I have many times—I'm overwhelmed with how deeply they must have loved each other to overcome the obstacles in their way and to ignore the ethnic and religious warning signs that, in retrospect, seem so obvious. But they were in love. As Mom wrote, "How grand it is to be alive when I know that in 3 weeks you'll be with me, never to be away from me again."

And they shared more than love. They also shared hopes and visions. Mom and Dad were dreamers. Not so much the Mom and Dad I knew, but the Mom and Dad I discovered in those letters, before the realities of life squelched many of those dreams.

Dad dreamed of writing, which he repeated over and over, referring to himself as "an artist in chains." Mom dreamed of pursuing a singing career. Dad even made contact with someone he knew at the San Francisco Opera and encouraged Mom to write, becoming irritated when she didn't follow through and urging, "Dearest, please stop smoking, you want your voice to be as beautiful as possible."

Love, hopes, and dreams nourished my folks when they got married, even though they didn't have much in the way of material possessions. Mom had her wedding gifts, including plenty of undergarments and nightgowns, which she listed in her letters. Dad had some stocks, which he sold to pay for his trip to Kansas City and to furnish their modest apartment. Other than that they were starting virtually from scratch ("I am poor and my future still uncertain other than a tremendous capacity for hard work.").

I don't know what would have come of those dreams if...well. Mom and Dad got married on July 16, 1933. The next year, on April 6, 1934, I was born.

Every now and then I find myself, in spite of myself, thinking about their life together had it not been for Baby Carlos. But Baby

Carlos arrived, changed their lives, and probably doused some of their dreams.

Obviously I wouldn't want to change the fact that I came along. But sometimes I can't help thinking about my folks' dreams and wondering what if...

EPILOGUE

60

A Family Legacy

It's been more than a quarter of a century since my family—the family in which I grew up—came to an end. The Cortés family goes on, but it's very different—more extended, less conflicted, more dispersed, less angst-ridden.

For me, it's been a wonderful and eventful time. Laurel has brought me three decades of love, joy, and companionship. We've won trivia contests, been in a movie together, rafted for two weeks down the Colorado River through the Grand Canyon, and visited all seven continents, including Antarctica.

My daughter, Alana, has carried on a Cortés family tradition, becoming a third-generation family graduate of UC Berkeley. For six years she taught in an elementary school Spanish-English dual-language program, and has since become a superb teacher trainer for the Los Angeles Unified School District, specializing in the education of English Language Learner students.

She and her husband, Richard, have two daughters and live eighty miles away in Los Angeles. They anointed their daughters with double middle names honoring our Mexican family heritage: Amaya Paloma Cortés Lawton and Tessa Grace Cortés Lawton. Alana seems to have inherited the sardonic Cortés sense of humor, informing me that she couldn't resist giving me a Politically Correct granddaughter—Amaya P.C. Lawton.

My brother, Gary, and his wife, Debby, still live in Kansas City. Their oldest daughter, Rita, is also there, while their other two kids have moved away, Natalie to a Chicago suburb, Marc to Portland.

Gary and Debby's three children graduated from Pembroke-Hill, the coed private school formed when my alma mater, Pem-Day, merged with Sunset Hill, a local private girls' school. All three are married, two of them to Jews, and together they have four kids. Two of Gary's kids keep kosher.

The family has kept alive Dad's flame of community involvement. Gary became president of Beth Shalom, Kansas City's Conservative Jewish synagogue. When the Kansas City Hispanic Chamber of Commerce named him Man of the Year, I gave the banquet address.

Rita has taken over the construction company, the fourth generation of our family to be part of it, quite an achievement in this world of mergers, bankruptcies, and family feuds. The business name remains Hoffman-Cortés, but the company's stationery has been redesigned twice. In the first iteration, the big bold blue *C* in the logo dwarfed the smaller, lighter gray *H*. Dad must have smiled. Later, the *H* and *C* became the same size, parallel and set into a dark background. This may have brought a glint to Granddad's eyes.

When Dad moved into the Villa Ventura in 1984, Gary and Debby bought and remodeled his house. So when I visit Kansas City I sometimes stay there, the home that's been part of my family since my folks built it in 1952.

I get to Kansas City at least once a year. Usually it's for family, but sometimes it's for professional reasons or special occasions. In the spring of 1989 I went back to Kansas City to receive Pembroke-Hill's Distinguished Alumnus Award. Few of my classmates showed up for the Saturday afternoon cocktail party and ceremony. But, after all, I hadn't bothered to see most of them since graduation in 1952.

Thirteen years later, in April 2002, I enjoyed a nostalgic Kansas City week teaching creative writing to sixth and eleventh graders as Pem-Hill's Writer in Residence. I spent one evening with four of my former classmates at the Carriage Club, where I read them earlier drafts of the Pem-Day chapters from this autobiography. My best Kansas City friend was there, Barnett Helzberg, who's now enjoying retirement after selling his national jewelry store chain to Warren Buffett. And Jim Tinsman, our senior class president. Paul Hunt, the football team tailback and Missouri state dash champion. Mark Nardyz, the star point guard of our basketball team. Except for Barnett, the only other Jew in my graduating class, they were leading members of the high school "in" crowd.

All were surprised by my observations. Even my buddy Barnett, who confirmed Pem-Day's social and religious divide, didn't know of my tortuous journey. But in those olden days we didn't let it all hang out, even with friends.

Paul, Jim, and Mark had no idea of the gulf between the "ins" (mainly athletes and country club boys) and the "outs." That's not surprising. They were decent guys, "ins" who probably didn't even realize how much the "outs" were being excluded...or that there even were "outs." But that's what often happens when you're an "in."

Or maybe, as they suggested, we "outs" may have imagined a more impervious divide than actually existed. But that's what often happens when you're an "out."

For nearly four hours I read and we talked, drank, and laughed. As the evening wore on, I could feel the remains of my teenage angst departing, erased by these new relationships being fostered after half a century.

Two weeks later my class held its fiftieth reunion. I didn't go back for it. I'd already had mine.

* * *

Professionally, the painful multicultural experiences of my youth, my serendipitous relocation to California, where diversity became central to my personal and professional life, and the unexpected family moments of my post–Kansas City days have continued to infuse my national and global activities. After I retired as a history professor in 1994, I launched a new career as an independent writer, public lecturer, and diversity consultant, giving talks and workshops in forty-eight states (all except Delaware and West Virginia), and in Europe, Asia, Australia, Canada, and Latin America. I became part of the faculties of the Harvard Institutes for Higher Education, the Summer Institute for Intercultural Communication, and the Federal Executive Institute, while I team-teach diversity leadership courses each fall at the University of Maryland.

Along the way I've collected a bunch of honors. Two honorary doctorates. Several book and article prizes. Numerous awards for scholarship, teaching, and public service from my university and from national organizations.

In 2000, the publication of my book, *The Children Are Watching: How the Media Teach about Diversity*, led to an offer to work with an animated children's series, then in its planning stages. That show, *Dora the Explorer*, made its debut later that year on Nickelodeon cable network. Ultimately I became creative/cultural advisor for *Dora* and its sequel, *Go, Diego, Go!*, and shared in the National Association for the Advancement of Colored People's Image Award. The NAACP statuette resides handsomely in my office. Whenever I'm introduced for one of my talks, my Dora and Diego affiliation draws a far bigger response than any of my degrees, publications, or other awards. Those two little Latinos have given me my ultimate street cred.

I'm not much into psycho-babble, but maybe—just maybe—my work with diversity is a natural (inevitable?) extension of those Kansas City years. My family life constantly creeps into my talks and workshops: growing up straddling the borderline between Judaism and Catholicism; eating dinners in a Spanish–Yiddish crossfire; living with family ethnic warfare between Mexico and eastern Europe; surviving the summer of '54; sharing the Chicano movement with Dad; experiencing Israel and Rome with Mom and Grandma; and chanting the blessing at Natalie's Bat Mitzvah. Maybe those experiences and the retrospective insights I've gleaned from them have honed my insights into the complexities of diversity and nourished the analytical multicultural muscles I now use as a professional.

It all began to come together on a sultry July 2003 evening at Pacific University in Forest Grove, Oregon. That night I held a reading of early drafts of some chapters from this book. Present were faculty, interns, and students at the Summer Institute for Intercultural Communication, where I teach each summer. One was a former theater director, Dawn Davies, then an English language teacher living in South Korea.

Afterward Dawn suggested that my story could make a good one-person play. I informed Dawn that I had never written a play, but Dawn graciously offered to help me if I would give it a try. Well, nothing ventured...So I began writing the play, and later I began performing it.

I call the play *A Conversation with Alana: One Boy's Multicultural Rite of Passage*. It is structured around an hour-long conversation between me and my daughter, Alana—represented on stage by an empty chair. I share with her my Kansas City coming-of-age experiences, while also responding to her questions and comments.

The play has become surprisingly successful, considering that I'm neither a playwright nor an actor. I've performed it more than

one hundred times from Los Angeles to Boston, from Seattle to
Miami, mainly at conferences, universities, and high schools. Of
course, I've done it several times in Kansas City.

Often there are post-performance discussions, sometimes last-
ing more than an hour. Questions about my family and how I
wrote the play. Testimonials from audience members, relating
their own family experiences.

Sometimes people share deeply personal revelations and make
commitments to action as a result of seeing the play. A young
Mexican American woman said she was now determined to interview her parents about how their families came to the United
States. A Jewish student who, like me, had never mentioned
his religious identity to his classmates, now decided to wear it
proudly. A young Muslim man, engaged to a Christian woman,
vowed that he would go home that night and, for the first time,
talk with his fiancée about the raising of their children-to-be, a
subject they both had studiously avoided.

I think Mom, Dad, Grandma, and Granddad would be happy
that their stories are helping others.

* * *

One final note. In addition to running the construction company,
Rita supervises family real estate investments, in which we're all
involved. Each year we gather in Kansas City for the annual family business meeting. This guarantees that all three generations of
the Carlos and Gary clans get to spend extended time together at
least once a year.

During those Kansas City trips I usually visit Rose Hill. Sometimes Alana and her family go with me; sometimes a larger Cortés
contingent; sometimes just Gary and I; sometimes Laurel and I.
On occasion I go out there alone.

On those solitary visits I share news and memories with my
family. Stories about Laurel, Alana, Amaya, and Tessa. King
Arthur and the Israel trip with Grandma. Gin rummy and cigars

with Granddad. Opera and the Pope with Mom. Chicano politics and the polo club with Dad.

I think I know what they'd say. I think they'd all be relatively happy with how things have worked out. They wouldn't totally agree with the other one; but they never did. At least they'd each find things that could bring them comfort...in their own ways.

61

A Letter to Alana

Dear Alana,

There you have it. My story. My family's story. Your family's story.

So what comes next?

Gary and I have talked about it. Someday one of us will call to say "Hi, bro," and then realize that "bro" isn't around anymore to pick up the phone. One of us will be the last of the ben Avraham brothers.

Laurel and I, too, have discussed what comes next. At first we assumed that we would be buried next to each other. But where? In Riverside? Why? Most of our friends are either gone or will be departing about the same time we do. So we gave up that idea. In fact we gave up the whole idea of being buried together.

I know this might offend your sensibilities, but please hear me out. Laurel and I love each other enough that we don't need to end up lying alongside each other to make our love last. Besides that, we've each got a family tradition and, with advancing age, traditions become more important.

Laurel's mother and father were cremated, their ashes then taken by boat from San Diego harbor and scattered at sea. Some of Laurel's siblings are planning to do the same thing. She'd like to join them. It's the right thing.

And me? Well, when the time comes, I'm going home to Kansas City to be with my family, in Rose Hill Cemetery. I've already bought a plot.

Please, no complaints about how far away I'll be from you. You're busy working and raising your own family in Los Angeles. I don't want you feeling guilty about not driving out more often to Riverside—those eighty miserable, bumper-to-bumper miles—just to visit my grave.

Then there's something else: the annual family business meeting in Kansas City. That's when you can visit me. Once a year is plenty.

But when you do, please humor me. During those flights to Kansas City, why don't you reread this story. And when they're old enough, read it to your little Amaya and Tessa.

If you do that, I think you'll find that each visit will be different, that you'll understand more and more what your family did and why they did it, the pleasure and pain that life brought them, and the legacy they left for you and your little girls.

If you do that, I think you'll grow to know them in ways that you didn't while they were alive. I'm not sure whether this story and those visits will make you like your family any better. But I think you'll grow to love them even more.

And when you go out to Rose Hill, don't go directly to my grave. First, go see Grandma and Granddad Hoffman, who loved you so much even though—maybe I shouldn't say it, but I've got to—who adored you even though you were their only non-Jewish great-grandchild. They'd be very proud of what you've done and who you've become.

Then take that seventy-five-yard walk over to the rose garden where Mom and Dad are buried. Those agonizing seventy-five yards. Agonizing to Mom because she had to make a final choice between Dad and Granddad, those two men she loved so much. Agonizing to Grandma because it shattered her dreams of a complete family plot. Agonizing to Dad, torn between triumph and grief. Maybe your visits will help them rest a little easier.

You can bring them all up to date on the family. You can tell Mom about Rita's beautiful singing voice and how she's keeping up Mom's musical tradition. Maybe Mom will even forgive her for keeping kosher. Tell Dad about your involvement in the education of immigrant children. He'll be delighted, but don't be taken aback if he makes some wry comment. Tell Granddad that his little construction company is still going strong after nearly a century, now headed by the fourth generation of our family, and that his name lives on. Let him know that what he started from scratch still thrives. Just don't expect him to smile.

Maybe most importantly, tell Grandma that she finally has her family plot...Rose Hill. We're not all buried right next to each other, as she dreamed, but we're not that far apart and there are more of us to come, since Gary, Debby, Rita, and I have plots. At first she might not accept the idea of Rose Hill itself as a family plot, but stay with it. Keep repeating that idea, even if Grandma objects in Yiddish. She'll come around. She always does.

Tell them all that the family is strong. That we get together every summer and take care of the real estate businesses. That we enjoy each other, take pride in one another's accomplishments, and don't fight.

Then, when my time arrives, come on over to my plot. I'll be waiting for you. Section 6, Lot 33, Grave Number 3. It'll be great to see you.

Love,
Dad

About the Author

Carlos Cortés is professor emeritus of history at the University of California, Riverside. His books include *The Children Are Watching: How the Media Teach about Diversity* and *The Making—and Remaking—of a Multiculturalist*, and he has edited three book series on Latinos in the United States, totaling 106 volumes. He is the general editor of *Multicultural America: A Multimedia Encyclopedia* (Sage, forthcoming). Cortés has written film and television documentaries, appeared as guest host on the PBS national television series *Why in the World?*, and is creative/cultural advisor for Nickelodeon's Peabody award–winning children's television series *Dora the Explorer* and its sequel, *Go, Diego, Go!*, for which he received a 2009 NAACP Image Award. Cortés has lectured widely throughout the United States, Latin America, Europe, Asia, Australia, and Canada on the implications of diversity for education, government, private business, and the mass media. His memoir, *Rose Hill*, has been adapted into a one-person autobiographical play, *A Conversation with Alana: One Boy's Multicultural Rite of Passage*, which Cortés has performed more than one hundred times around the country.

Inlandia Institute

Inlandia Institute is a lively center of literary activity located in Riverside, California. It grew out of the highly acclaimed anthology *Inlandia: A Literary Journey through California's Inland Empire*, published by Heyday Books in 2006.

Inlandia Institute strives to nurture the rich and ongoing literary traditions of inland Southern California. Its mission is to recognize, support, and expand literary activity in the Inland Empire by publishing books and sponsoring programs that deepen people's awareness, understanding, and appreciation of this unique, complex, and creatively vibrant area.

For more information about Inlandia Institute titles and programs please visit www.heydaybooks.com/book_category/inlandia or www.inlandiainstitute.net.

HEYDAY
into California

About Heyday

Heyday is an independent, nonprofit publisher and unique cultural institution. We promote widespread awareness and celebration of California's many cultures, landscapes, and boundary-breaking ideas. Through our well-crafted books, public events, and innovative outreach programs we are building a vibrant community of readers, writers, and thinkers.

Thank You

It takes the collective effort of many to create a thriving literary culture. We are thankful to all the thoughtful people we have the privilege to engage with. Cheers to our writers, artists, editors, storytellers, designers, printers, bookstores, critics, cultural organizations, readers, and book lovers everywhere!

We are especially grateful for the generous funding we've received for our publications and programs during the past year from foundations and hundreds of individual donors. Major supporters include:

Anonymous; Evenor Armington Fund; James Baechle; Bay Tree Fund; S. D. Bechtel, Jr. Foundation; Barbara Jean and Fred Berensmeier; Berkeley Civic Arts Program and Civic Arts Commission; Joan Berman; Peter and Mimi Buckley; Lewis and Sheana Butler; California Council for the Humanities; California Indian Heritage Center Foundation; California State Library; Keith Campbell Foundation; Candelaria Foundation; John and Nancy Cassidy Family Foundation, through Silicon Valley Community Foundation; Center for California Studies; Compton Foundation; Nik Dehejia; Frances Dinkelspiel and Gary Wayne; George and Kathleen Diskant; Donald and Janice Elliott, in honor of David Elliott, through

Silicon Valley Community Foundation; Euclid Fund at the East Bay Community Foundation; Eustace-Kwan Charitable Fund; Federated Indians of Graton Rancheria; Mark and Tracy Ferron; Judith Flanders; Furthur Foundation; The Fred Gellert Family Foundation; Wallace Alexander Gerbode Foundation; Wanda Lee Graves and Stephen Duscha; Alice Guild; Coke and James Hallowell; Carla Hills; Sandra and Charles Hobson; G. Scott Hong Charitable Trust; James Irvine Foundation; Kendeda Fund; Marty and Pamela Krasney; Guy Lampard and Suzanne Badenhoop; LEF Foundation; Judy McAfee; Michael McCone; Joyce Milligan; National Endowment for the Arts; National Park Service; Steven Nightingale; Theresa Park; Patagonia, Inc.; Pease Family Fund, in honor of Bruce Kelley; The Philanthropic Collaborative; PhotoWings; Alan Rosenus; The San Francisco Foundation; San Manuel Band of Mission Indians; Savory Thymes; Hans Schoepflin; Contee and Maggie Seely; Sandy Shapero; William Somerville; Martha Stanley; Stanley Smith Horticultural Trust; Stone Soup Fresno; Roselyn Chroman Swig; James B. Swinerton; Swinerton Family Fund; Thendara Foundation; Tides Foundation; Lisa Van Cleef and Mark Gunson; Marion Weber; Whole Systems Foundation; John Wiley & Sons; Peter Booth Wiley and Valerie Barth; Dean Witter Foundation; and Yocha Dehe Wintun Nation.

Board of Directors

Getting Involved

To learn more about our publications, events, membership club, and other ways you can participate, please visit www.heydaybooks.com.

ECO-FRIENDLY BOOKS
Made in the USA